THE WRECK OF THE
FAITHFUL
STEWARD
—— ON ——
DELAWARE'S
FALSE CAPE

THE WRECK OF THE
FAITHFUL STEWARD
— ON —
DELAWARE'S FALSE CAPE

MICHAEL TIMOTHY DOUGHERTY

THE
History
PRESS

Published by The History Press
Charleston, SC
www.historypress.com

Front cover, background: Background painting by Kevin Fitzgerald; shipwreck image by artist and engraver P. Gilbert, 1833. *Courtesy of the National Maritime Museum, Greenwich, London.*
Back cover: Image of the Cape Henlopen light, 1780. *Courtesy of the Library of Congress Rare Book and Special Collections Division, Washington, D.C.*; *inset*: George III guinea coin (1779) recovered on Coin Beach. *Author's collection.*

First published 2023

Manufactured in the United States

ISBN 9781467153560

Library of Congress Control Number: 2022949637

Notice: The information in this book is true and complete to the best of our knowledge. It is offered without guarantee on the part of the author or The History Press. The author and The History Press disclaim all liability in connection with the use of this book.

For Angela and Jack

CONTENTS

FOREWORD

This book on the tragic loss of the ship *Faithful Steward* off the coast of Delaware in 1785 is methodically researched and reliably sourced. In it, author Michael Timothy Dougherty offers readers a nuanced understanding of the political, cultural and economic drivers of late eighteenth-century migration from the British Isles to the newly formed United States.

Dougherty takes a penetrating look at the motivations of those involved in the two-way trade from Derry to Philadelphia, from freedom-seeking migrant families to ship crews willing to gamble everything to realize the enormous profits that the trade had to offer. He also takes time to examine the immigration debates of that era—just like today, thought leaders spent considerable time discussing the positive and negative effects of human movement on both sending and receiving countries.

As a sea story, this book gives us a vivid and graphic understanding of the hardships and hazards that migrant families experienced at sea, including inadequate food and appalling cooks, compact and filthy living quarters and poorly trained ship crews.

Dougherty creates an immersive experience when describing the mechanics of wrecking in a wooden ship; it was a brutal event, and the hierarchy of survival was cruel, as few children and women remained alive in the violent hurricane surf that pounded the Delaware shoreline. It is a testament to the horror of that experience that immigrant James McEntire (the passenger through whom we witness this historic voyage) remained psychologically affected by what he saw even forty-six years after the event.

Personally having sailed and motored over five thousand miles in a ketch-rigged sailboat and aboard numerous research vessels, I found Dougherty's study of the dynamics of wave action and navigational hazards presented by the ever-changing shoals and beaches to be among the most compelling chapters in the book.

The sands of Delaware's "False Cape" continue to yield relics from the remains of the *Faithful Steward*. These artifacts serve as a reminder of the opportunity—and peril—that the New World offered generations of migrants seeking freedom on these shores.

Bruce F.C. Thompson
Retired Assistant State Underwater Archeologist (1989–2016)
Maryland Maritime Archeology Program (MMAP)
Maryland Historical Trust (MHT)

ACKNOWLEDGEMENTS

I thank the kind and talented people who assisted in the production of this book: artist Kevin Fitzgerald of Newark, Maryland; maritime archaeologist Bruce Thompson of Annapolis; readers and editors Kevin Green and Kathleen Pepper of Alexandria, Virginia, as well as Drs. Virgil and Anca Nemoianu of Bethesda, Maryland; researcher Sister Elizabeth Corrigan of Belfast, Ireland; photographers Jessica and Dave Vermont of Ocean Pines, Maryland; acquisitions editor Kate Jenkins at The History Press in Charleston; and the staff of the Principle Gallery in Alexandria.

1

THE AMATEUR EMIGRANT

The weather in the year 1785 was unusually cold and dry. Planters in Virginia woke in late April to find their crops crusted with frost. Rivers in New England carried ice all the way into June. Ponds and lakes across the French countryside dried up, and farmers were reduced to slaughtering their cattle and selling them wholesale. Water levels dropped so low in the Seine and the Rhine that barges and boats could not make it over the shoals. In July, an English correspondent wrote, "Such weather was never known here as we have had these six months past, no more than two days rain during the whole time."[1] It stopped raining in Mexico, too. With no maize crop, they would remember this as "The Hunger Year."[2]

The weather had some gifts to give, however. It brought "extremely fine"[3] conditions to the northern coast of Ireland, a place commonly enshrouded in clouds and rain. The abundant sunshine brightened the walled city of Londonderry (better known as Derry), lighting up the surrounding hills and the waters of the River Foyle, which curved around the foot of the town in a deep arc.

The Derry walls had four gates. One was the Shipquay Gate, which stood at the bottom of a steep cobblestone street. The gate could be understood as a kind of portal from one world to another, because it was here that generations of Irish emigrants would pass on their way to board ships for America, leaving the Old World for the New.

On July 9, an emigrant by the name of James McEntire walked below the Shipquay Gate for the final time. Together with his parents, eight sisters,

A view of Londonderry on the River Foyle. *National Library of Wales.*

a brother and other family,[4] McEntire boarded a three-masted American sailing ship headed for the port of Philadelphia.

The quay between the gate and the wharves along the river had the bustle of a country fair. Sailors, dockworkers, ship chandlers, merchants and passengers of all ages moved among heaps of luggage and cargo in bundles, boxes and kegs of all sizes. People talked, laughed and yelled, babies cried, carts trundled back and forth and dust rose into the clear air. One emigrant describing a similar scene wrote that many were unfamiliar with sea travel,

> *yet there was a display of cheerfulness that was remarkable—as if their minds were made up for whatever might betide, or that the novelty of their situation had produced an excitement which cheered them in the hour of parting from their own home, shores, and the friends they loved. Mothers were sitting giving nourishment to their infants—but they had their husbands with them; children were eating or playing, but they were not separated from their parents; and in no instance was a saddened countenance to be seen amongst them.*[5]

This would be McEntire's first great adventure. He had high hopes. "I was," he said, "a suitable person to seek the wilds of America.…I saw in imagination…a country where the banner of freedom waved proudly; a country where heroes lived, where genius expanded to full perfection; where every good was possessed. I saw, or thought I saw, another paradise, a new and flowery land."[6]

When the writer Robert Louis Stevenson later envisioned "the ideal emigrant," he thought the "emigrant should certainly be young" and "should offer to the eye some bold type of humanity, with bluff or hawk-like features, and the stamp of an eager and pushing disposition."[7] We do not know exactly what McEntire looked like. We do know that he was taller than most and physically strong. And he was indeed young, twenty-two years old and "just emerging into complete manhood and active life."[8] We can imagine him as one of those fair, freckled, sturdy young men who were standard issue among the Scots who had settled on the Ulster plantations in the north of Ireland, a people known as Ulster Scots, or later, Scots Irish.

McEntire's understanding of America and his good opinion of it were shaped by many sources. The Scots Irish had migrated there in a steady stream for decades. The stories that came back to Ireland from the Eastern Seaboard and the frontier hit the high points of the experience: plenty of food, decent wages, cheap land, religious freedom and a government that was both tiny and benign. Those arriving in the United States immediately following the Revolutionary War exulted in the thriving markets, the low prices of grain and livestock and the lifting shadows of religious and class distinctions.

Such accounts excited Irishmen of every variety, who had watched the war unfold with admiration and rejoiced in its successful conclusion just two years before. But the stories and letters home often passed over the discomforts, the diseases, the climate, the insects, the snakes and the enormous primordial forests. There was concern from leaders in the United States that aspiring immigrants did not fully understand what they were in for and greater concern about the kind of people who would be attracted to their shores. In Great Britain and Ireland, officials were alarmed that valuable working people were being allowed to wander off the land and into the arms of a nation with natural resources that were imperfectly understood but appeared boundless. America, they feared, would be a rival. It was just a question of when.

The ship that would carry the McEntire family to America was named *Faithful Steward*. It was new,[9] built in the summer of 1783 in the suburbs

Young emigrants seldom returned home. *Library of Congress.*

of Philadelphia, where over a dozen active shipyards were located and where most maritime tradesmen lived.[10] It would have been built to very high standards. By the time of the Revolution, generations of professional shipbuilders had been honing their craft along the banks of the Delaware River. Philadelphia native Tench Coxe bragged that his city made the best ships on earth and from the choicest materials, including "live oak, and red cedar of the Carolinas and Georgia."[11] Some said that American ships were preferred by English merchants because they could "be had cheaper and better than those that are built in England."[12]

The *Faithful Steward*'s owners described the ship as "high between decks, and a remarkable good sailer."[13] Walking along the Derry quay, McEntire saw a "noble vessel of 350 tons"[14] that towered over the coastal craft and homely local fishing boats tied up alongside. Transatlantic sailing ships had an aura all their own. Apart from their imposing size—they were the biggest moveable objects that most people had ever seen—they were complex, expensive and often beautiful creations, a highly evolved fusion of utility and art.

Irish emigrants were not sailors but small farmers, weavers and laborers, or tradesmen from country towns. They often traveled in extended family groups ranging in age from the elderly to the newest baby. They knew that ocean crossings were perilous, long and uncomfortable. Few of them knew how to swim: it was a skill that seemed "only to be calculated for people of mean condition, such as watermen, sailors, to whom their employment has made the arts of swimming and diving in some measure necessary."[15]

Shipowners advertising for emigrant business sought to reassure them, usually through serial promises about the excellence of the captain's character, the quality of the food and water that would be served to them during the voyage and the size and speed of their vessel. The *Faithful Steward* "sails remarkably fast," said notices in the local papers, "all passengers shall be treated with tenderness and humanity, and . . . provisions of every kind shall be laid in, and of the best quality."[16] The "conduct of the captain to his passengers last year," they declared, "makes it unnecessary to point out his humanity."[17] Advertisements also tended to exaggerate. McEntire had been told the *Faithful Steward* was 350 tons.[18] But an advertisement from the previous year stated that it was 300 tons.[19] Still another said the ship was only 250 tons.[20]

Shipowners often implied that their vessels were specifically designed to carry people. The classic but ambiguous phrase found in dozens of shipping advertisements was that a ship "is in every respect well calculated for the passenger trade."[21] However, the ships shuttling between Derry and American ports were merchant ventures, engaged in either "freight or passage," carrying whatever or whomever would fill the ship soonest and get it moving profitably back in the other direction. So, Derry ships carried emigrants of all kinds—"passengers, redemptioners and servants"[22]—and exported cargo of all kinds, whether it was linen, butter, beef, pork, silk, oatmeal, boots, shoes or hats. Sleeping berths for emigrants between decks and in the hold were temporary fixtures, made up of rough boards nailed together for the outbound trip. And those sleeping berths were infamous. Stacked two or three high, emigrants lay on mattresses filled with straw open to bedbugs and lice, in spaces that might be as little as two feet wide and eighteen inches high. On arrival in the Port of Philadelphia, the filthy berths would be dismantled and thrown out to make room for cargo on the return voyage.

The *Faithful Steward*, whatever its actual tonnage might have been, would pack in more than 360 people for the 3,200-mile voyage to Philadelphia.[23] The usual emigrant fare was four guineas per person,[24] which represented months of wages for a laboring man.

Leaving for America. *Wikimedia Commons*.

The ideal time for a Derry emigrant to arrive in Philadelphia was early spring. The transatlantic voyage west could be a little rougher at that time of year, but it was faster than a summer passage. On landing, emigrants intending to settle on the frontier would have longer days to set about the business of clearing land and planting crops. It would also give Irish emigrants time to acclimate to American weather, which was essential: the warmer summer days in Derry are sixty-seven degrees, while those in Philadelphia are typically eighty-seven, almost equal to the highest temperature ever recorded in the north of Ireland.

The captain of the *Faithful Steward* was an Irishman named Connelly McCausland. He owned a one-third interest in the ship.[25] A prominent member of the Ulster gentry, Captain McCausland lived on a family estate at Streeve Hill, located in the scenic countryside near Derry.[26] McCausland originally intended to set sail on May 20[27] but had postponed the ship's departure well into the summer.

The optimal time for an Atlantic voyage had slipped away. It was not until July 9 that the *Faithful Steward* left the quay in Derry, riding the ebb tide on the smooth waters of the River Foyle. As it traveled north into the broader reaches of the bay known as Lough Foyle, the spare green hills of Donegal rose to the left, while the salt marshes and farms of Limavady kept pace on the right. The ship eased through the narrows between Greencastle and Magilligan Point and began to feel the swell of the North Atlantic, which surged cold and green over the black rocks at the base of Inishowen's cliffs. The *Faithful Steward* packed on sail to clear the land.

"I stood on deck to view the fading shore," McEntire later said. "I was leaving my native home forever; I was leaving my companions of early time; I was leaving the hills, the plains, the groves, the streams, where I had wandered a thousand times, and when it had been my childish employ to stand, to gaze, to think and be happy."[28]

With smooth sailing, the *Faithful Steward* would reach the port of Philadelphia in seven weeks. That would put it off the American coastline toward the end of August, at the height of hurricane season.

2

GOD SENDS MEAT AND
THE DEVIL COOKS

In the days following the *Faithful Steward*'s departure from Derry, one of the most famous men on earth was making final preparations for his own voyage to Philadelphia. That was Benjamin Franklin, who was leaving Paris after nine long years of service as the first U.S. ambassador to France. Dr. Franklin would not sail with an ordinary merchant captain but with Thomas Truxtun, an expert navigator and fighting captain who had commanded several American privateers during the Revolutionary War, when he gained a reputation for hurling himself at larger armed opponents and capturing valuable prizes. With the peace, Truxtun had returned fully to the merchant trade, and his four-hundred-ton *London Packet* was preparing to rendezvous with Franklin across the English Channel off the Isle of Wight. Known (and somewhat feared) for his punctuality, Captain Truxtun had warned Franklin that he must be on board the ship no later than August 1.[29]

The usual cost of a passage on Truxtun's ship was 35 gold guineas for each cabin passenger plus 15 apiece for servants—prices that would have astonished a Derry emigrant. Being wealthy and an experienced ocean traveler, Dr. Franklin reserved the entire cabin for himself, so that he "might not be intruded on by any accidental disagreeable company."[30] He would lay out 280 guineas for himself, five passengers, three servants and tons of baggage that included his papers, books, a printing press and 128 jugs of his favorite mineral water.[31]

On this trip, Dr. Franklin would write a long letter, "Maritime Observations," to a member of the French Academy of Sciences.[32] Focused

Benjamin Franklin studied images like these from *The Art of Swimming* to improve his skills. *New York Public Library*.

on nautical topics, the letter features Franklin's distinctive blend of applied science and practical advice, covering everything from anchoring systems to a new design for soup bowls that would not splash their scalding contents on the laps of diners when a ship was moving in heavy weather.[33] Franklin was comfortable on the water; he had been an aquatic creature since he was a boy and promoted swimming as a way to stay physically fit and avoid "the slavish terrors many of those feel who cannot swim, when they are obliged to be on the water even in crossing a ferry."[34]

As Franklin was making his rendezvous with Captain Truxtun, the *Faithful Steward* was over 1,200 nautical miles from Derry and well into the North Atlantic. It was not sailing at the "remarkably fast"[35] speeds promised by its owners but was instead ambling along below five miles an hour and averaging about 50 miles a day.

The emigrants on board the *Faithful Steward* were enjoying the voyage. James McEntire remarked that the "weather continued to be very beautiful, while the ship, in all its grandeur, floated on the surface of the deep, and approached with majestic ease and celerity the place of our destination."[36] The air and sea temperatures were mellow, in the middle seventies.[37] At night, those too restless for sleep climbed on deck to find the stars close and seeming to drape the ship in a silvery light.

The *Faithful Steward* sighted numerous vessels bound for America, and several others crossed its path on their way to ports in Britain and Europe. On August 1, *Faithful Steward* closed with the *Ashley*, which was sailing from Jamaica to London. Captain McCausland was probably interested in the *Ashley*'s estimate of their position. It seems he was not carrying a sextant and chronometer and so did not know with certainty how far to the west his ship had sailed. Both devices were relatively new pieces of technology in 1785, handsome to look at, painstakingly made and expensive to own. They were not common equipment on merchant ships, whose captains usually determined longitude through celestial navigation, using an old-school quadrant and consulting the lunar tables in well-thumbed copies of the *Nautical Almanac* published by the Astronomer Royal.

As Captain McCausland exchanged information with Captain Castle of the *Ashley*, the passengers marveled at the sight of a ship so close alongside in the wilderness of the open ocean. Benjamin Franklin said of a similar meeting,

> *There is really something strangely cheering to the spirits in the meeting of a ship at sea, containing a society of creatures of the same species and in the same circumstances with ourselves, after we had been long separated and excommunicated as it were from the rest of mankind.... When we have been for a considerable time tossing on the vast waters, far from the sight of any land or ships, or any mortal creature but ourselves (except a few fish and sea birds) the whole world, for aught we know, may be under a second deluge, and we (like Noah and his company in the Ark) the only surviving remnant of the human race.*[38]

The two ships soon parted ways and lost each other over the horizon. When the *Ashley* made London at the end of August, Captain Castle told *Lloyd's Register*, the paper devoted to shipping news, that his ship "on the 1st Inst. spoke the Faithful Steward McCasling, from Londonderry to Philadelphia, in Lat. 44. N. Long. about 36 E. all well."[39]

James McEntire recalled that everyone on the *Faithful Steward* "no doubt anticipated a quick and delightful voyage"[40] to the New World. While moderate winds and calm seas prevailed, the emigrants were nevertheless coming to understand in full that the voyage was really a test of endurance. There was a geometry to transatlantic crossings in wooden sailing ships that did not change from one decade to the next between the seventeenth and nineteenth centuries, because the essential ingredients were the same: a mass of people in a confined space for a period of roughly two months in a vessel that relied wholly on the wind for propulsion, riding a watery medium that itself was in constant motion. Seasickness was a common scourge that settled on some passengers and not on others; it was so arbitrary that it seemed to resemble luck. A few might be prostrate for the entire voyage, nibbling at bland foods and "bitterly cursing Columbus for having discovered America."[41] Others would feel nauseated for a couple of hours or days and then suddenly well as their inner ears adapted to the rhythms of the ship.

Typically, the first to bounce back from seasickness were children. The dim world of steerage was not for them; they were attracted to the squares of sunlight from the companionways and scrambled up to the main deck to try out their sea legs. They watched with open wonder as the crew climbed the rigging far overhead and marveled at the immensity and smooth lines of the canvas sails at work. The braver ones wanted to see the water splashing against the hull and had to be watched closely as they leaned over the ship's rail to have a look. Children often made up a third to a half of the emigrants aboard ship, and everyone knew it, because they were a constant source of noise, drama and amusement.[42]

Few sailing ships engaging in the two-way trade between Derry and Philadelphia were rigged with portholes.[43] The *Faithful Steward* did not have them. As a result, there was little air movement and light between decks. In such ships, the steerage area where emigrants lived and slept was seventy-five feet long, twenty-five feet wide and only five and a half feet high. Historian Edwin Guillet wrote, "On either side of a five-foot aisle were double rows of berths made of rough planks; and each berth, designed to accommodate six adults, was ten feet wide and five feet long." The narrow aisle between berths "was congested with their baggage, utensils, and food."[44]

Emigrants were expected to provide their own bedding aboard ship and would slide straw mattresses into these unfinished, flimsy rectangles and wriggle in, pulling a couple of blankets behind them.[45] They called steerage "a loathsome dungeon" or the "Black Hole of Calcutta" and had a thousand ways to describe how the place smelled, "a horror" being the most common.[46] The air was stifling. The veteran traveler Thomas Mooney would later advise his cousin Patrick, "Choose a berth as near to either of the hatchways as you can, and let it be the lowest berth of the tier....The average air of the hold of a ship, with some two hundred and fifty people packed below, is about fifty per cent weaker or less nourishing than the air on the deck of the vessel....If you sleep up high you will be obliged to inhale the hot, exhausted breath of the whole company near you, which…is as bad as poison to your lungs."[47]

There was no real privacy for emigrants in steerage. This came as something of a shock for country people who were not used to living in proximity to large numbers of strangers. Women and children were sometimes segregated from men for reasons of modesty. "Lavatories, except of the most primitive nature, were never available"[48] and often consisted of nothing more than a shared bucket that needed to be emptied topside. Some people, wrote historian Donald MacKay, "took to relieving themselves in the darkness of the hold, for there were never enough chamber pots, and often none at all."[49]

Another source of discomfort was the inability to keep clean. The ship did not carry enough fresh water to spare for bathing. Captain McCausland might have hoisted barrels of ocean water to the main deck for passengers to sponge off, but the salt stayed on the skin and over time was an irritant. Fresh water was always a concern for Irish emigrants. They expected to get two quarts to a gallon of clean water for drinking and cooking each day.[50] The ideal was to have collected water from a spring or well for storage in hardwood casks, "sweet and tight, of sufficient strength, and of wood properly charred inside, and capable severally of containing not more than 300 gallons each."[51] But the water was often bad, "for the casks were filled from the river in which [a ship] happened to be anchored, and if enough was left for a second voyage they did not take the trouble to renew the supply."[52] One passenger complained that when the water on his ship "was drawn out of the casks it was no clearer than that of a dirty kennel after a heavy shower of rain; so that its appearance alone was sufficient to sicken one. But its dirty

There was little privacy or room in steerage. *Library of Congress.*

3

A FINE LEVEL SHORE

To reach the port of Philadelphia, Captain McCausland of the *Faithful Steward* needed first to locate the entrance to Delaware Bay. Merchants and insurers in Philadelphia wanted to make certain that he and every other shipmaster could find it with ease. That is why they had constructed a lighthouse on a tall sand hill on the southern tip of the bay, a long, curving tongue of sand known as Cape Henlopen. The sand hill was called "the Great Dune," and some called the lighthouse "The Old Man of the Atlantic."[63]

The idea of building a lighthouse on Cape Henlopen was first seriously entertained by the Pennsylvania Provincial Assembly in November 1761. With commerce "increasing, and frequent accidents befalling the shipping,"[64] the Assembly quickly set up a lottery to raise £3,000, naming some of the leading merchants of Philadelphia as managers of the effort. When the lottery fell short of its target funding, it was decided to issue bonds to make up the remainder. It was not until September 1763 that the Assembly had enough money in hand to go forward with the project.[65]

Philadelphia's lottery scheme—indeed, the entire lighthouse effort from funding to construction—bore an uncanny resemblance to efforts already underway in New York, where the Provincial Congress had authorized a £3,000 lottery of its own in May 1761 to build a light at Sandy Hook. The two port towns were and would remain commercial rivals. New York boasted one of the largest natural harbors in the world and was close to the Atlantic: one could stand on Staten Island and see the open ocean to the right and the protected waters of New York Harbor to the left. By

The emigrants aboard the *Faithful Steward*, like those who came before them and those who would come after, were fixated on remaining healthy. There was no medical doctor on board who could treat them on the journey. Travelers knew the long period of confinement and inactivity aboard ship would reduce their physical assets, which they would need in the months after landing. Said Mooney, "Be provided too with a little salts, senna, or castor oil, one or two doses of which should be taken during the voyage, and especially *one on arrival* in America, will be a *most valuable preservative of* your *health*, which in the New World, is your *only* fortune."[62]

baked bread cut in slices that held up well in the long weeks aboard ship. Said Franklin, "The ship biscuit is too hard for some sets of teeth. It may be softened by toasting. But rusk is better; for being made of good fermented bread, sliced and baked a second time, the pieces imbibe the water easily, soften immediately, digest more kindly and are therefore more wholsome [*sic*] than the unfermented biscuit. "[58]

Thomas Mooney told his cousin, "As to sea-store, you must be guided, Patrick, by your pocket: a poor man will have a poor wedding." He advised,

> *Eggs can be kept during a long voyage by rubbing them with butter or suet, and bedding them,* on their ends, *in salt or oatmeal, packed in a close box; milk also may be kept in the following way:—get forty or fifty small bottles, or pop jars; boil a couple gallons of pure new milk, and throw in a couple of handfulls of brown sugar and when cool, fill your bottles or jars to the cork; keep them as cool as you can, and use* one bottle a day; *if the milk fails, an egg beaten up will answer to the same purpose—it will supply your tea or coffee with an* ameliorator. *Strong coffee or tea, unmixed with salt or eggs, used for several days at sea, tends to produce costiveness, and prepares the body for fever, cholera, or any other infectious sickness that may lurk in the dirty clothes of the passengers.*

Mooney added, "You should have a basket with a lid and padlock, to hold and preserve your provisions sweet during the voyage; if you pack them in a chest, they will sour and become mouldy. This is true of all but the eggs, which should be kept air tight in small boxes."[59]

Another veteran of the Atlantic crossing suggested "a stock of good thick cake ginger bread, gingerbread nuts, and oranges and apples a very good thing at sea. You can sometimes swallow a nut, or suck an orange when you would turn in disgust from anything else."[60] Still another recommended,

> *Acids of all descriptions—that is, those used at table—are not only serviceable at sea, but particularly grateful to the palate. Of vinegar, therefore, as the most common, there should be ample store; pickles likewise of various descriptions; but above all, lemons or the juice of them. For this kind of acid there can be no proper substitute; it counteracts the effects of salt diet, allays sea-sickness, and forms occasionally a very refreshing and invigorating beverage.*[61]

appearance was not its worst quality. It had such a rancid smell that to be in the same neighborhood was enough to turn one's stomach; judge then what its taste must have been.…The stink it emitted was intolerable."[53] Attentive ship crews would drop a pound of charcoal into a barrel of water and let it settle for an hour, which improved it.

Irish emigrant vessels usually provided food for passengers, comprising "staples of the provisions trade," which included beef, ship bread, unlimited supplies of oatmeal and a pound of butter or a pint of molasses a week.[54] The beef was salted and stored in barrels. It needed to be cooked, and that posed another kind of problem. There were no proper stoves aboard the ship on a scale adequate to feed hundreds of people at dinnertime. Instead, there were usually one or two cooking ranges placed above-deck, wooden boxes lined with bricks and holding coal fires behind open grates, which some called a "camboose." This was often managed by one of the ship's crew. "The worst thing in ordinary merchant ships," wrote Benjamin Franklin, "is the cookery. They have no professed cook, and the worst hand as a seaman is appointed to that office, in which he is not only very ignorant but very dirty. The sailors have therefore a saying, *God sends meat and the devil cooks*."[55] Such cooks could turn out soup that was "merely stinking water in which stinking beef had been boiled, which no dog would taste unless he was starving." Or perhaps tea "boiled as black as can be" and "scarcely suited for the stomach of a rhinocerous."[56] Robert Louis Stevenson remembered that the tea and coffee on his ship were "surprisingly alike.…I could distinguish a smack of snuff in the former and dishcloths in the second. As a matter of fact I have seen passengers, after many sips, still doubting what had been supplied them."[57]

Like James McEntire, many of the emigrants aboard the *Faithful Steward* were members of large, extended families and relatively prosperous members of the Irish middle class. They did not do things in haste; they had prepared for their removal to America for months and understood the food served aboard ship would be of low quality, repetitive and dull; they also knew they would likely be seasick. They put considerable thought into how they intended to feed their families on the voyage and spent considerable time and money getting their provisions ready, including purchases of tin pots, pans and small "ovens" to quickly heat up their food at the charcoal grates on deck.

Franklin advised ocean travelers to pack their own food to supplement the ship's rations. He suggested good tea and ground coffee, chocolate and wine, cider and rum; sugar, almonds, raisins and lemons; and rusks, a crisp, twice-

The Philadelphia waterfront. *Library of Congress.*

comparison, Philadelphia was well up the Delaware River and not less than eighty-eight nautical miles from the Atlantic.[66] Tench Coxe wrote somewhat defensively, "The distance of Philadelphia from the sea, has been made an objection by some, and the closing of our river by the ice…from three to nine weeks almost every winter, yet there are occasional openings which give opportunities for fleets of merchantmen to go out and come in."[67]

The Assembly formally committed to building the lighthouse in October 1763 and appointed a body of commissioners to oversee the work.[68] The newly installed colonial governor of Pennsylvania, John Penn, granted a patent of two hundred acres at Cape Henlopen for construction.[69] The commissioners, with the assistance of a local ship pilot, selected a site some forty feet above sea level on the edge of the Great Dune, a mile south of the Cape and a quarter mile inland. The light would be exposed to ships making landfall from the Atlantic and to those coming down the bay, a full 270 degrees of useful aid to navigation.

While New York's eight-sided lighthouse at Sandy Hook was being constructed of undressed, rough granite rubble, the Philadelphia commissioners decided to do it one better. The walls of their octagonal lighthouse would be constructed of blocks of granite in the ashlar style, with each piece dressed to fit tightly against its neighbors and laid horizontally for a formal appearance. It was an expensive style, the kind of work usually performed by highly skilled masons. The best stone to be found was up on the Brandywine River near Wilmington. Known as Brandywine Blue Gneiss, it was a powder blue granite that gave off a slight sparkle when freshly cut. The burly men working in the Delaware quarries called it simply "blue rock." Tons of it were extracted and carried by boat down to the build site on the cape,[70] where it was split into "rather small"[71] blocks to make for precise edges on the tower's outer surface. The tick-tick-tick of masons finishing the stones with their points, punches and tooth-chisels filled the air around the Great Dune for months as the tower took shape. Transient sailors and locals from the nearby town of Lewes visited the site to relax on the sand and check on the builders' progress: it was always interesting to watch skilled laborers at their work.

In November 1765, the *Pennsylvania Journal* wrote, "It is with pleasure we can inform the public, that the elegant Light-house building on Cape Cornelius (commonly called Cape Henlopen) will be very soon lighted for the direction of shipping."[72] By September 1767, the lighthouse had been completed.[73] The base of the tower was twenty-six feet across, and at ground level its walls were six feet thick. At the top of the tower, seventy feet into the air, the walls were three feet thick.[74] A wooden staircase led upward to eight interior levels, with windows facing the sea and the countryside. The lantern room was enclosed in glass supported by iron framing. The cupola atop the lighthouse ended in a flourish with an overlarge weathervane, visible from sea. The "handsomely built"[75] lighthouse was one of the most imposing public structures in colonial America and would ultimately take on an iconic status, serving generations of mariners from all over the world.

In future years, inspectors from the Treasury Department's Light House Board would make infrequent, sandy hikes out to the Henlopen light and find much to complain about: leaks in the lantern far up in the tower; leaks in the roof below; the lack of supplies for the keeper; the absence of posted instructions for tending the lamps and reflectors; the dubious motives of the man who delivered oil to fuel the light, his billing practices and the quality of his summer and winter oils; and on and on. What they did not complain about was the tower itself, briefly noting that it was "well built."[76]

The General Assembly did its best to protect its investment. In 1773, it decreed that anyone who burned or destroyed the lighthouse would be fined £1,000 "and suffer three years imprisonment, without bail or mainprize, and

Cape Henlopen in 1780: a place of skeletons. *Library of Congress.*

be whipped once in every year, during such imprisonment, at the common whipping post, with any number of lashes, well laid on his bare back, not exceeding thirty nine."[77]

That specific and draconian law did not prevent a catastrophic fire that consumed the interior of the lighthouse during the Revolutionary War. It is speculated that local Patriots intentionally gutted the light to make navigation difficult for British warships like the forty-four-gun *Roebuck*, which lurked off the cape hoping to capture American merchantmen.[78]

The more interesting story told later in the *New York Times* was that the British sent a foraging party ashore under the command of an officer who asked the lighthouse keeper, Hedgecock, if he would sell them some of his cows:

> *"I'll give you no cows, but if you don't get out of here I'll give you some bullets!" declared Hedgecock. The keeper had ears attuned to the echoes of the Liberty Bell drifting down the Delaware from distant Philadelphia. The gold-laced British official was angry. He retorted that he could send a few bullets himself, and retreated to his longboat. Old Hedgecock, smoking his pipe in the doorway of his eight-sided tower, contemplated the seven-foot-thick stone walls thereof without excitement. They could well defy the [marine cannons] of 1780. A landing party rather than the expected bombardment surprised the keeper and his assistants. It was well for them that fully a mile separated the lighthouse from the sea in those days.... There was time for them to seek shelter for themselves, and very likely for*

the disputed cows, in the deep pine woods behind the lighthouse.…The
British, finding nothing at hand to confront the landing party, took out their
spite on the lighthouse. They set its interior wood-work and wooden stairs
merrily ablaze. Down from the top hurtled the oil hand-lamp which was
the Henlopen Light of that period, together with the circular table on which
it rested, and the tiny reflector.[79]

Cape Henlopen did not show a light for years following the fire. It was not until February 11, 1784, some five months after the official end of the Revolutionary War, that port authorities in Philadelphia informed the public that "lights are again fixed in the light house on Cape Henlopen.…In future, the greatest attention will be observed in rendering so necessary and important a directory both useful and satisfactory to navigators."[80]

If there was an upside to the fire, it might have been the introduction of new lighting equipment. The latest innovation in lamp-lighting came around 1780 by way of François Pierre Ami Argand, a chemist and hot air balloon enthusiast from Geneva.[81] His design, using cylindrical glass chimneys to burn high-grade cotton wicks soaked in whale oil, reduced smoke and soot and produced light six to ten times brighter than ordinary candles.

While Argand's lamp made for a better light, the remaining challenge was to *throw* that light to the horizon. To make that happen, a large, cone-shaped parabolic reflector, usually made of copper plated with silver, was placed directly behind the lamp, facing out to sea. The mirrored surface of the reflector concentrated light rays to a single point, creating a crisp, concentrated beam, visible from miles away. Lighthouses often featured numerous Argand lamps arrayed in an arc to cover the approaches to shore. Although effective, fixed arrays like those at Cape Henlopen did not offer unbroken 360-degree-light but instead threw out spokes of light, creating a hazard. Navigators were warned, "At great distances, in *fixed* lights, when you are in the direction between the axes of the adjoining reflectors, the light is frequently glimmering and feeble, but a small change in the position of the ship brings you again into the brighter beam of the reflector, one of which, it will be understood, is only in sight at a time."[82] Depending on who you talked to, the eight lamps of the Henlopen light were visible seventeen to thirty-four miles at sea or better in good conditions,[83] but it is probable that ships at extreme ranges could sail blind for considerable distances between the direct beams of light from the tower.

The Argand lamp represented a major safety enhancement for ocean travelers. But in the lighthouse business, the adoption of next-generation equipment was remarkably slow, and the upkeep of existing equipment was left either to bureaucrats who exhibited the casual negligence common to their kind or to the personal initiative of the lightkeeper. Treasury inspectors touring coastal lighthouses noted with displeasure that reflectors were "different in nearly every lighthouse which was visited by the board, and in numerous instances they differed materially on the same frame. The majority of these were spherical, and not parabolic, in shape,"[84] which resulted in a weakened, blurry light.

With the Cape Henlopen lighthouse coming back online in 1784, its wooden innards and lighting equipment replaced, a new keeper was hired. His name was Abraham Hargis. He was fresh from service in the Continental army, where he held the rank of lieutenant in a Pennsylvania regiment.[85] Perhaps the best kind of lighthouse keeper was something of a worrier, attuned to small details, a willing slave to schedule, routine and repetitive tasks. To his credit, Hargis seemed to have all these qualities. Not every keeper was as diligent. Lighthouse inspectors complained, "Few keepers give their entire attention to the lights under their charge; many follow other vocations, which require them to be absent for days at a time from the lights, leaving them to be attended to by some incompetent member of the family, or perhaps, as there are numerous instances, by servants."[86]

Lighthouse work could be isolating. It was of course a nocturnal job, performed out on the edge of civilization, as few people lived on the beach. But the air was usually good and free of mosquitoes and there was little heavy labor involved. If Abraham Hargis wanted to socialize, he could cut across the cape and walk to Lewes about three miles away. Lewes was a small and simple place, a "dreamy, drowsy, old-fashioned, bayside town"[87] of clapboard and shingle homes weathered by breezes off the Atlantic. It might provide companionship but not much in the way of excitement.

For the lightkeeper's entertainment, the waters off Cape Henlopen offered the never-ending spectacle of maritime trade passing by, inbound for Philadelphia or outbound to almost anywhere: Bermuda, Amsterdam, Boston, Jamaica, Charleston, Nevis, Glasgow, St. Kitts, Rhode Island, the Bay of Honduras, London, Lisbon, Barbados, St. Christophers, Cork, Plymouth, Gravesend, Bristol. The trade was carried by sloops, schooners, brigs and ships with names like *The Two Friends*, *The Swan*, *Lark*, *Bachelor*, *Success*, *Betsey and Polly*, *Friend*, *Jenny* and *Globe*.[88]

Walking the gallery deck atop the Henlopen tower, Hargis was some 115 feet above sea level. From that height, his sight line to the horizon was 13 miles in every direction. The oceanfront and countryside around the light was bucolic and unassuming; this was not the northern Irish coast of James McEntire's youth, with its headlands of gray rock thrusting into the sea. The landscape here, said one early Dutch explorer, was "beautifully level."[89] A later ship passenger would describe it as "a fine level Shore."[90] When the Dutch arrived in the 1630s, they called it "Swanendael," the "Valley of the Swans," where the birds were so numerous they blocked the sky and the world's best oysters were "piled up heap upon heap, until islands they attain," in this "noblest of all lands."[91]

If Hargis looked to the west from his tower, he could see across Lewes and up the southern shore of the Delaware Bay as it receded into the distance toward faraway Philadelphia. That shoreline was known to the Indigenous Lenni Lenape tribe as Sickoneysinck, the "place where there is a gentle sound from the movement of things."[92] To walk the narrow beach there was to encounter the horizon at maximum strength and to lose all sense of scale; nothing broke the plane of miles of open water and sky that seemed emphatically divided as by a ruler. The beach was fringed by colonies of pale saltmarsh cordgrass, backed by marshes and meadows that ran unbroken to stands of mast-straight loblolly and gnarled pitch pine and dry hummocks of low bayberry, holly and wax myrtle.[93] In the slanted light of dawn, the low country along the Delaware Bay glowed gold and green.

Looking south, Hargis would see the marine forests, grasslands and fields of the mainland ending abruptly in the shallow waters of Rehoboth Bay, separated from the ocean by a narrow strand of beach, dunes and scrub running straight as an arrow to the southeast. On a clear winter day, Hargis could make out a thin blue line cutting across the strand, with waves breaking silent and white on a fan of sandbars reaching into the Atlantic. That blue line was the Indian River Inlet, eleven miles away and well within reach of the Henlopen light. The inlet extended from ocean to bay, the sole connection between the two, and it was untamed, roaming north and south along the strand when storm surges cut new passages through the dunes to the back bay and silted in the old channels. A traveler observed, "These inlets are so influenced by the action of storms, and their shores and locations so changed by them, that the cattle may graze to-day in tranquil happiness where only a generation ago the old skipper navigated his craft."[94] The *American Coast Pilot* warned mariners early and often that passage through the Indian River inlet was "fit only for small vessels that draw not more than 6 feet water."[95]

The landscape around the Indian River inlet was composed of low sand knolls sculpted by the wind. Pitch pine, huckleberry bushes, myrtle shrubs,

A rare view from Indian River to the beach in 1788. *Library of Congress.*

seagrass and the occasional prickly pear cactus grew along and behind the primary dune line facing the ocean. In the ochre hollows of the dunes, the sound of the surf was muted, and small deer and rabbits moved with equal quiet. The flats where the ocean breached the dunes were littered with blue and white shell fragments from whelk, oysters, periwinkles and clams. Nothing here was permanent, and nothing grew very tall. An 1862 nautical chart created by Baltimore artist and cartographer Fielding Lucas featured a "view of the coast from Indian River to Cape Henlopen," depicting the landscape as seen from three miles out at sea. To the north, the Henlopen light stood guard at the entrance to the Delaware Bay, on the shoulder of the Great Dune. Moving south, sandy bluffs gradually fell away to a low series of hummocks and isolated stands of trees, diminishing to a thin line of beach at Indian River that hardly rose above the surface of the sea.[96]

There is no science that can forecast the movement of sand by wind and waves. It is fair only to say that the sand is in constant motion. Lightkeeper Hargis knew this because he could hear the patter of grains against the windows of his house below the Henlopen tower whenever the wind came up, and it was a daily chore to sweep fresh sand from his porch. He knew what every keeper at the cape would know: that the Great Dune itself was moving slowly to the southwest and leaving the lighthouse behind.

The transport of sand in the water around Indian River inlet is invisible to the eye. Ocean waves striking the shore at an angle create littoral currents running parallel to the beach. Such currents, notes science writer Cornelia Dean, "can move a veritable river of sand in one direction or another as winds shift along the coast, especially in storms."[97] When hurricanes and northeasters spin up from the south, the shape of the beach itself can be transformed in a matter of hours. The summer beach, broad, lofty and rounded like a loaf of bread, can be reduced to a slender, tilted hardpan in as little as two tide cycles, the sand seemingly gone forever. "But the sand is not actually lost," says Dean:

> *In a process still not fully understood, the surf transmutes this sand into bars that, in turn, break the storm waves' force before they reach the beach. In a big storm one, two, or even three sandbars may form off the beach, each one dissipating the waves' energy so that when they hit the beach they run up, sink into the porous sand, and ooze back out, taking little sand with them. Meanwhile, as wind and wave winnow away the lightweight particles and blow them inland, the remaining heavier bits of broken shell, rock fragments, and grains of dark red garnet or other minerals act as armor for what lies beneath.*

In this dynamic, the beach "has simply used its sand resources in its own defense."[98]

The rapid formation of sandbars in the nearshore environment around the Indian River inlet creates a variety of hazards. Sandbars are close to the surface and set up plunging waves, which have a "total integrated force"[99] double that of spilling waves. As the swell contacts the submerged bar, it walls up into a vertical face with an accelerating crest that arcs out and down and strikes the seafloor. The entrained air captured by the falling wave is spun forward and pushed to the bottom, with the resulting bubble plume carrying sand up as far as the surface before the next wave enters the impact zone.[100] This combination of sandbars and fast, hard waves is dangerous to vessels large and small. A shoal can bring a deep-draft vessel to a full stop and hold it there as plunging waves batter away at the hull and deck. Smaller coastal craft can pitchpole end over end or broach and be rolled toward the beach.

Sand shoals are not confined to the area close to the beach. The *American Coast Pilot* warned in 1857 that the waters from Cape Henlopen south to the Virginia line were "studded with shoals, lying at a distance off, from 3 to 6 miles, to the nearest point of land," adding:

> *The coast in this vicinity is dangerous for large vessels navigated by persons not well acquainted with it. Vessels supposing themselves in this vicinity, after striking 11 and 12 fathoms of water, should keep the [sounding] lead going, and keep a bright look-out. In the day-time,*

large vessels should not approach nearer the land than 8 or 9 miles, with the trees just in sight from the deck; nor at night, even in clear weather, when coming from the southward.[101]

The advice to navigators seeking to enter Delaware Bay at Cape Henlopen was emphatic and would not vary over 150 years, whether it was to jobbing merchant captains of the eighteenth century or to commanders of U.S. Navy missile frigates in the twentieth. Navigator Edmund March Blunt told shipmasters in 1833 they "should be careful not to approach nearer than 12 fathoms water, until they have got into the latitude of said Cape,"[102] and the U.S. Coast Pilot said in 2022 that "a deep-draft vessel should not approach the coast closer than depths of 12 fathoms until sure of its position."[103]

These instructions were clear enough. But in the 1700s, the southern coast of Delaware featured an optical illusion that lured sailing ships into shoal water close to shore. It was a wood of white oak trees on Fenwick Island below the Indian River Inlet. They were old-growth trees, remnants of the primeval forest that once covered the coastline, standing as high as 150 feet above the ground. Like all white oaks, they threw their limbs wide and had a bushy appearance. From the sea, this mass of tall, broad trees looked something like the Great Dune at the mouth of Delaware Bay. Ships coming up the coast from the south saw the trees and assumed it was time to begin a port turn left into the bay. But they were not even close; the bay was still some twelve miles off to the north. Early mapmakers wanted to warn sailors of this dangerous illusion. Those mapmakers were Dutch. They gave the wood the strange name Cape Henlopen.[104]

The name was explained in exasperated and sarcastic detail by John Penn in a 1743 lawsuit against Charles Calvert, fifth Baron Baltimore. The Penns and Calverts had argued for years over the proper location of Maryland's northern border, which passed through Fenwick Island. In his court briefing, Penn wrote:

Cape Henlopen lay…to the south of Cape Cornelius…at a place called Phoenix or Fenwick's Island. The name of that Cape Henlopen *is a* Dutch *Word. The translation of it is, Cape Run-away, or Cape Vanishing, or Cape Disappearing. And it was a* significant *name, and carried sense and meaning in it. For, tho' the land was higher there, and there were likewise, upon Fenwick's Island, very great high trees, both which contributed to make the land there look bold, like a cape, or promontory, or head land, when out at sea; yet, when sailors, upon the faith of that appearance, stood in to it, it answered its name, it proved deceitful, it run away, it vanish, it disappeared, as they approach it nearer and nearer, and in fine, was found to be indeed, far without it, and south of that mouth or entrance.*[105]

Over time, sailors (who are precise in many things but capricious in bestowing names on objects and places) began calling the woods on Fenwick Island the False Cape, while transferring the name Cape Henlopen to the actual southern cape of Delaware Bay.

From atop the lighthouse on Cape Henlopen, if lightkeeper Hargis looked due east, he could easily spot the Hen and Chickens, a long shoal trailed by a smaller set of bars to the south. Portions of it were covered by as little as three to five feet of water. The Hen and Chickens was so close to the shipping lane around the cape that buoys were placed on it to warn ships off.

Looking directly north, Hargis could see the beaches and low dunes of Cape May, New Jersey, twelve miles in the distance. Extending south from Cape May and nearly blocking the entrance to Delaware Bay was a large network of shoals known as the Overfalls. The water here was as shallow as five to fifteen feet.[106] When the wind was on these shoals and the tide was setting up against them, the Overfalls were a disorienting, lawless jumble of whitewater, with large waves hurling themselves against one another and vaulting straight into the air. A southbound ship fleeing before a hurricane or northeaster, making leeway and running out of sea room, had to squeeze between the Overfalls on the right and Cape Henlopen on the left, then skid to a stop behind the hook of the cape, to find whatever comfort the shallow waters near Lewes had to offer.

No one knows, and no one will ever know, how many ships were lost on the Overfalls. In the murk of a storm, a vessel could struggle and die there with no witnesses. One visitor described a dozen "green-coated, barnacle covered, skeleton-ribbed wrecks…embedded in the sands" of Cape Henlopen, adding:

Hundreds of bodies, washed in from wrecks, and without marks of identity, have been carried only a few feet from the water which stole their lives and placed in the sand. So rapidly did the colony of dead grow at one time that every rough blow would remove the crown of the sandhill they made and expose the bleached bones. While walking through this heavy sand we found exposed a thigh bone and bone of a forearm. There are no monuments to

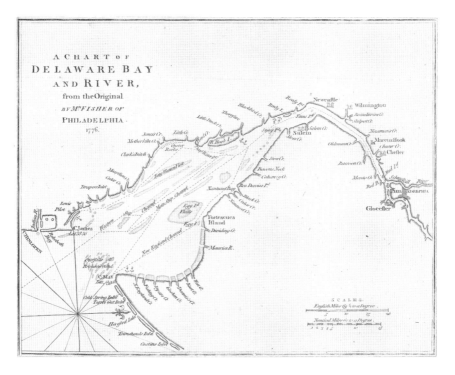

The dangerous shoals of the Delaware coast. *New York Public Library.*

perpetuate the names of the buried, and no mounds tell the wanderer where to pick his way and tread gently—only one great, large grave, with its several hundred dead.[107]

The way to Philadelphia was lined with shoals. Leaving Cape Henlopen, ships heading up Delaware Bay needed to navigate the Shears, Joe Flogger, the Brown, the Brandywine, the Breakers, the Cross Ledge, the Upper Middle, Bombay Hook, Dank's Bar and a half-dozen others.[108] There were no good charts of the route. One official of the infant U.S. Navy would report, "Many dangerous shoals having but a few feet of water upon them, and upon which numerous wrecks have occurred, are laid down from three to five miles from the truth, and the bay is in one part represented as *fifteen* miles in width, when it is actually but *seven*." He concluded, "There is no chart extant of the Delaware, deserving the name."[109]

Locals insisted that Delaware Bay was "far more dangerous…in windy weather, than the main ocean."[110] There was really nowhere to hide; the bay could be as much as twenty-five miles across, with no surface friction to slow the wind. The main shipping channel was far from shore and hemmed in on both sides by sandbars that ran for miles on a parallel track. In light winds, it could take hours for a sailing ship to ease by the Joe Flogger Shoal, buried and invisible in the dark waters of the bay. It was not until the bay narrowed to become the Delaware River that captains could begin to relax.

Many captains headed for Philadelphia had little interest in trying to understand the intricacies of navigating the Delaware Bay, no matter how well buoyed it might be. They would instead take on a local pilot outside the capes or in Lewes. Piloting was a serious business carried on by professionals; they were held in high regard in Lewes. Pilots included members of the Unalachtigo people, a branch of the Lenni Lenape who had lived in southern Delaware for thousands of years.[111] The Unalachtigo were known as "people who live near the ocean,"[112] and few pilots had a better understanding of the bay.

It was to this world—unassuming in appearance and seemingly docile, but full of tricks—that the *Faithful Steward* made its steady progress in the early weeks of August.

The Delaware Bay was as dangerous as the ocean itself. *Library of Congress.*

A diminutive, teetotaling Yankee adventurer named Nathaniel Bishop passed through this country in a canoe in 1874 on his way from Canada to Florida. In all his travels, Bishop met with a single serious accident. It was on Delaware Bay, when his little craft flipped over in heavy seas below Murderkill Creek. He wrote:

> *I struck out in an almost exhausted condition for the shore. Now a new experience taught me an interesting lesson. The seas rolled over my head and shoulders in such rapid succession, that I found I could not get my head above water to breathe, while the sharp sand kept in suspension by the agitated water scratched my face, and filled my eyes, nostrils, and ears. While I felt this pressing down and burying tendency of the seas, as they broke down upon my head and shoulders, I understood the reason why so many good swimmers are drowned in attempting to reach the shore from a wreck on a shoal, when the wind, though blowing heavily, is in the victim's favor.... The water shoaled; my feet felt the bottom, and I stood up, but a roller laid me flat on my face. Up again and down again, swimming and crawling, I emerged from the sea.*[113]

Bishop finished his story with an admonition: "At such a moment do not stop to make vows as to how you will treat your neighbor in future if once safely landed, but strike out, fight as you never fought before, swallowing as little water as possible, and never relaxing an energy or yielding a hope."[114]

4

A STRANGE HUMOR

On August 20, a Saturday, the *Faithful Steward* was six weeks into its journey and sailing under a full moon. The average transit time for a vessel between Derry and Philadelphia was seven weeks, so there was a rising expectation among the crew and passengers that they would soon be in soundings off the American coast.[115] The trip so far had been uneventful, not to say dull. James McEntire recalled that spirits were high, "the greatest harmony having prevailed among" the emigrants aboard ship.[116]

The morale of the passengers was boosted by the fact that many were blood relatives. There were at least nine immediate families on the *Faithful Steward*, including more remote kin who were collectively referred to as "cousins." In addition to James McEntire's family, there were Elliotts, Hepburns, Lees, Stewarts, Campbells and Calhouns.

The Elliotts "consisted of the father, five daughters and two sons, Simon and William."[117] The family's eldest son, John, was already in Pennsylvania on something of a scouting mission. His father had sent him over the previous year on the ship *Lazy Mary*, instructing John to write the family "to do some impossible thing" if he thought conditions were favorable for the family to emigrate. The senior Elliott felt the subterfuge was necessary because the authorities might try to press his younger boys into military service if it was discovered the family meant to leave Ireland. In time, the family received a note from John in which he said "that he had been unable to build himself a house and asked them to send theirs over to him." The Elliotts took the hint, sold their large family home in the north of Ireland and went to Derry to board the *Faithful Steward* in July.[118]

The Hepburn family had done something similar, the male members of the family leaving Derry in twos and threes, "attracted by the reports which reached them of the beauty and fertility of what was known as the 'New Purchase'—or more particularly the lands lying in the valley of the West Branch of the Susquehanna."[119] One of the Hepburn sons, Samuel, had been dispatched to settle affairs in Ireland and to bring his mother and sister to Pennsylvania. Being well off, they traveled in comfort as cabin passengers.[120]

The Lee and Stewart families were related to the Elliotts. The Lees were perhaps the most populous family on the ship. They included James Lee, who was twenty-six years old, "accompanied by his parents, three brothers, two sisters, a brother's wife, three uncles, three aunts, and thirty-three cousins."[121] Among his relations was Mary Lee , a woman of such captivating looks and graceful manners that she was known as "the Irish beauty," and a popular ballad would be written about her.[122] General Robert E. Lee, who decades later would lead the Confederate armies in the American Civil War, counted these Lees among his ancestors.[123]

These families were among the "249 passengers of respectability" on board the *Faithful Steward* who paid down the cost of their passage in advance.[124] They were carrying with them "a very considerable amount"[125] of cash in the form of gold and silver coinage[126] as well as personal property, such as "clothes, books, household furniture, and tools or implements of their trade."[127] They had sold off their tenancies, land holdings or business interests in Ireland in anticipation of buying acreage in Pennsylvania on which to farm, or to set up shop in one of America's growing towns.[128] They were skilled farmers, linen weavers, artisans and mechanics, what were commonly known as "middling people"[129] or "the middling class."[130] Most families were Presbyterian, the immediate descendants of the Scots who had settled on the plantations in the north of Ireland in the province of Ulster in the 1600s.

There were at least ninety-eight other emigrants sailing with the *Faithful Steward*.[131] They were not formally recognized as "respectable passengers" in the parlance of the day because they could not afford to pay the four-guinea passage to America.[132] Captain McCausland, however, was willing to make a deal to cover the cost. Before taking ship, stout laboring men, country tradesmen, young men[133] and unmarried girls were offered "a contract, called an indenture," in which they agreed to serve McCausland

Emigrant families on the move. *Library of Congress.*

for "a period of years in return for passage to America." On arrival in New Castle or Philadelphia, McCausland would then sell the indenture "usually to the highest bidder," with the purchaser now assuming the role of "master for the remaining period expressed in the indenture."[134] It was a lucrative side to the shipping business because captains and ship-owning firms could sell an indenture well above the actual cost of transport and provisioning for a servant, with profits ranging from six to sixteen pounds and all paid in cash.[135]

Though some regarded indenture as "a despicable trade…carried on by some of the more unscrupulous captains and their confederates on the American side,"[136] it was an old custom and often the only way that young, single, poor people—many of them native Irish Catholics whose principal language was not English but Gaelic—could get passage across the Atlantic. McCausland obviously saw nothing nefarious in the practice. On landing in Philadelphia in September 1784, he took out an ad in the *Pennsylvania Gazette* announcing, "Just arrived the ship Faithful Steward…from Londonderry, a number of healthy men and women servants and redemptioners, whose times are to be disposed of on reasonable terms, by Capt. McCausland, on board said ship, lying off Walnut street."[137]

Aside from indentured servants, the *Faithful Steward* carried individuals known as redemptioners. "The redemptioner, strictly speaking, was an immigrant, but on embarking agreed with [the captain] to be transported without an indenture and without payment of passage, and on landing in America to be given a short period of time in which to find relatives or friends to redeem him by paying his passage."[138] It was not just friends and relations who were interested in redemptioners; they were highly sought after by American employers because they were mature, skilled craftsmen who could help turn a profit.[139] Redemptioners were able to bargain directly with employers for terms far more favorable than those of indentured servants. It was common for a redemptioner to travel alone; once established in America's favorable labor market, he could buy passage for the remainder of his family.

While English, Scottish and Irish authorities were untroubled by the outmigration of surplus labor in the form of Gaelic teenagers and field hands, they watched the departure of middling folk from the British Isles with a growing sense of alarm. Over the years, they would denounce emigration as an "evil,"[140] a "fever,"[141] "a strange humor,"[142] a form of "madness,"[143] an "epidemic disease of wandering"[144] and "worse than a pestilence."[145] "Why," they asked themselves, "would such sober, honest, industrious and skillful people want to abandon civilized society for the wilds of the American continent?"

There was no single answer to the question. The root causes of emigration from Ireland to North America had their origins in the bewildering tangle of rebellion, civil war, conquest, sectarian violence, religious persecution and economic exploitation that extended from Queen Elizabeth's reign in the sixteenth century to that of King George III in the eighteenth. Perhaps the best that one could do was listen to the words of the Ulster Scots themselves. One minister offered these "reasons for the exodus… in a sermon delivered on the eve of the sailing of a ship [from Ireland to America]. 'To avoid oppression and cruel bondage; to shun persecution and designed ruin; to withdraw from the communion of idolators; to have opportunity to worship God according to the dictates of conscience and the rules of his Word.'"[146]

James McEntire's descendants would remember that his family was motivated

> *by the glowing accounts which from time to time reached them from across the briny deep, of a land of liberty, where the wicked landlord ceased from troubling, and the weary tenant might till his own soil, and rest and worship under his own vine and fig tree, none daring to molest him by demanding the lion's share of the proceeds of his toil, or make him afraid by tearing down*

his humble cot from over the heads of his defenceless wife and little ones, if,
on account of the providential failure of his crops, he should be unable to
meet his rent bills.[147]

For its part, the English government across this era viewed Ireland as both a threat and opportunity. Uprisings among the restive Gaelic population, which was uniformly Catholic and eternally plotting with foreign powers to overthrow the Protestant Crown, must be suppressed. In turn, the rich pastures and farmland of Ireland's northern counties were unproductive and must be managed to provide a good source of revenue; the land would be confiscated from the native Irish and divided among political allies and favorites loyal to the Crown. Over time, the English government would bungle its way through both dimensions of the Irish puzzle with social engineering projects, incentives, punitive laws, trade controls and, when necessary, the sword itself.

The establishment of the Ulster plantations on lands seized by the English government began in earnest in the first decades of the 1600s and gained momentum after the failed Irish Rebellion of 1641. Hundreds of thousands of English "colonists" settled there as tenant farmers, attracted by long leases at reasonable rates and a set of informal rules that would come to be known as the "Ulster Custom," which recognized the tenant's "right of occupation" to the land he leased and his right to sell that lease to another with the approval of the landlord. Importantly, if a tenant made improvements to the property—draining bogs, clearing land, adding walls and buildings—his selling price could be as much as fifteen to twenty times the annual lease.[148]

While it was not as secure as actual private ownership, the existence of the
Custom set Ulster farmers apart from most other Irish farmers because it
gave them twice the security: if they chose to remain in Ireland, there was
some possibility of advancing themselves; if they chose to emigrate, they had
something to sell that could finance the passage to America and help them
start a new life there.[149]

The Scots had been welcomed south to the Ulster plantations by the new landowning class of wealthy English loyalists, petty officials, soldiers and clerics from the Church of Ireland. The Scots began to arrive in numbers in the 1650s. "Its people of this period were tall, lean, hardy and sinewy. They were ignorant of high living and had good nerves and digestion. They were combative, and not easy to get along with to those who did not fall in with their ways."[150] They also possessed superb fighting skills, and it was anticipated that the Scots would help maintain order among the dispossessed Irish natives. The influx of Scots to the plantations reached its peak in the 1690s.[151]

In addition to having their lands confiscated, the Irish Catholics—who comprised some 70 percent of the overall population and 40 percent of those living in Ulster—were subjected to a series of Penal Laws intended "to deprive them of economic and political power and social position."[152] The Penal Laws issued in spasms from the English government, reaching a crescendo under the reigns of William III and Queen Anne in the late 1600s and early 1700s. In the main, the Penal Laws were designed to "prevent the future growth of Popery"[153] and to that end banished Catholic priests from Ireland. They also mandated that observant Catholics who were unwilling to publicly denounce their faith could not practice law, "hold any public employment or place of profit or trust," inherit land, vote, teach school, send a child overseas for a religious education, own "any arms and ammunition," keep Catholic holy days or marry a Protestant with property over £500. Catholics were expected to pay double taxes if they did not swear fealty to the Crown and renounce their faith and to pay double the rate for support of the militia.[154] Pilgrimages made to one of St. Patrick's sacred sites by vast numbers of Catholic Irish were presumed to be "riots" as a matter of law.[155] In his usual pointed style, the Irish statesman Edmund Burke described the Penal Laws as "a machine as well fitted for the oppression, impoverishment, and degradation of a people, and the debasement in them of human nature itself, as ever proceeded from the perverted ingenuity of man."[156]

The Scots arriving on the Ulster plantations were Presbyterians whose faith was distinct from that of the Anglicans who made up the elite class of landowners in Ireland. Both, of course, were Christian, but the theology, organization and scriptural emphasis of the Presbyterians placed them outside the Anglican Communion represented by the Church of Ireland, which was "identical except in name with the Church of England."[157] The Anglican church, led by the English monarch, pursued policies over long years to create a "Protestant Ascendancy" in Ireland, but the Presbyterians were not considered members of the Ascendancy. Instead, they were regarded as "nonconformists" or "dissenters." To their surprise and displeasure, the Ulster Scots found themselves subject to many of the same Penal Laws applied to the Catholics.[158] Among other indignities and restrictions, the "Presbyterian minister was expected to preach only within certain specified limits, and was liable to be fined, deported, or imprisoned. He could not legally unite a couple in marriage, and at times he could preach only by night and in some barn."[159] It "was penal for a person of [the Presbyterian] persuasion to teach a school, or to hold the humblest office in the State."[160]

Both Presbyterian and Catholic tenant farmers in Ireland were obliged to support the Church of Ireland and its clergy through annual tithes, which functioned as a 10 percent tax on the "profits of lands, the stock upon lands, and the personal industry of the inhabitants."[161] Historian Maurice Bric explains that while tenant farmers were accustomed to supporting their respective churches, the yearly surrender of cash, crops, product or livestock to provide income to a remote Anglican clergyman who frequently had neither church buildings nor a congregation in the neighborhood was a burden of a different order. Compounding the problem was the inconsistent and subjective valuation of tithes, which were often collected by middlemen known as "proctors" or "tithe-jobbers" who arrived on farms with printed "tithe tables" setting rates on things like potatoes, wheat, barley and oats.[162] As the face of this "hotchpotch" system,[163] tithe-jobbers were among the most hated men in Ireland. The farming class nodded with appreciation at the story of the proctor who in 1763 "was seized by near one hundred persons, who…put him on horseback and carried him near half a mile; made part of a grave and threatened to bury him alive."[164]

One of the principal features of the Ulster plantation scheme was that nothing about it prompted landlords to remain on the land with their tenants or to reinvest any portion of the rents they collected back into the communities that worked the land. The plantations were spoils of conquest and treated as such by large numbers of the Ascendancy class, whose estates ranged from hundreds to thousands of acres. The elites were "absentee" landlords, and the common understanding was that most spent their time living in "luxury and dissipation in London and at the court."[165] Historian Bernard Bailyn observed, "Though the Anglo-Irish landowners who continued to live in Ireland led lavish and profligate lives and did little to improve the condition of the peasants, they were at least witnesses to the miseries of the laboring population and were susceptible to personal appeals for relief. But many of the largest landlords in Ireland were permanent absentees; their drainage of capital from the island was understood to be crippling the economy."[166] One emigrant concluded that most of the misery in the Old World could be traced to government-supported monopolies "whereby sets of men are permitted and aided by the public laws, to get possession of the…proceeds of the labour, of the great multitude around them; and, gathering this wealth into enormous masses, the great majority of these privileged people *waste* it in utter dissipation, demoralizing the people by bad example, and destroying the *capital* which should be placed in reproductive operation for their future support."[167]

The full effect of absenteeism was felt when the leases granted to many original Presbyterian tenants began to expire around 1717 and 1718. Those who had spent a generation improving their farms and fields found their rents "usually doubled and frequently tripled"[168] by their landlords, who set "rents as high as possible…without regard to the true value of the lands, or the goodness of the [existing] tenant."[169] This was known as "rack-renting." For many Ulster Scots, it was the final straw: to the spiritual harm of the Penal Laws was joined the material harm of tithes and excessive rents. In 1718, the Presbyterian minister James McGregor, remembered as the "Moses of the Scotch Irish,"[170] took ship with "a large part of his congregation [and] sailed for America."[171] He would not be the last minister to gather his flock and leave; "many Presbyterian clergymen actively promoted emigration to the American colonies, likening the exodus to the biblical flight from Egypt."[172]

Irish fortunes were also being shaped by other English policy choices dating back to the seventeenth century. In the mid-1600s, "Irish land was chiefly used for pasture, and Irish wealth was derived from the export of cattle, meat, butter and cheese to western English ports. The English landowners complained and the laws of 1665 and 1680 prohibited the importation of all this Irish produce into England."[173] The Irish were also barred from shipping these products to English colonies unless they were first unladed in English ports or carried in English ships. This effectively destroyed the trade. "Yet the Irish did not despair," wrote historian Patrick Weston Joyce. "Driven from cattle-rearing, they applied themselves to other industries, especially that of wool, for which the country is well suited. In those times Irish wool was considered the best in Europe [and its manufacture] was rapidly rising to be a great national industry, which was carried on almost exclusively by the Protestant colonists. But this, too, was doomed. The English cloth dealers, taking the alarm, petitioned the Crown in 1698 to have it suppressed," and the following year, heavy export duties and other trade restrictions were placed on Irish woolens by the Irish and English Parliaments. "The woollen mills ceased to work," and tens of thousands of "Irish Protestants— all prosperous working people—were immediately reduced to idleness and poverty by it; the Catholics, of course, sharing in the misery so far as they were employed…and 20,000 Presbyterians and other Non-conformists left Ireland for New England."[174]

The frustration of the Irish with their profound commercial and political subordination to England—a condition that looked and felt unnatural, even surreal—would be summarized generations later by the rebel Wolfe Tone, who wrote:

> *The present state of Ireland is such, as is not to be paralleled in history or fable: Inferior to no country in Europe in the gifts of nature, blest with a temperate sky and a fruitful soil, intersected by many great rivers, indented round her whole coast with the noblest harbours, abounding with all the necessary materials for unlimited commerce, teeming with inexhaustible mines of the most useful metals, filled by 4,000,000 of an ingenious and a gallant people, with bold hearts, and ardent spirits; posted right in the track between Europe and America, within 50 miles of England, 300 of France; yet with all these great advantages, unheard of and unknown, without pride, or power, or name, without ambassadors, army or navy.* [175]

To avoid conflict with landowners in England, the Crown had long signaled that the Irish should turn their talents to the manufacture of linen.[176] Linen had been a part of Irish dress for hundreds of years, but there was nothing intuitively attractive about making it a national industry. Compared to wool, it was laborious, slow and less valuable. Its biggest advantage was that the English did not regard linen as a major manufacture and were not likely to get in the way. An abject and reluctant Irish delegation appeared before the House of Lords in March 1704 and explained that Ireland would dedicate itself to the linen trade if England was willing to support and protect its market.[177] The Lords agreed, and thus the central planners of the English government—what businessman John King later described as a "base herd" of "designing sophists" and "sensual Nabobs"[178]—succeeded through trade restrictions in steering the Irish into a singular reliance on linen to supplement the incomes from their farms. It would create a great national industry and make Irish linen among the most sought after on earth, but it would also invite financial disaster among the middling class who relied on the trade.

The four horsemen of the apocalypse that visited Ireland throughout the eighteenth century were crop failures, deep declines in the export market for linen, food scarcity or famine and new outrages in rack-rents. They all seem to have arrived together about the time American dissatisfaction with English rule was growing by the day. Bernard Bailyn writes, "In 1770 the absentee Earl of Donegall demanded fees for renewing leases on his

BOY AND GIRL AT CAHERA.

The poverty of the native Irish astonished generations of visitors. *Wikimedia Commons*.

estate in Country Antrim that were three or four times annual rents, an innovation that touched off a wave of rioting" in the Ulster plantations. "And in the midst of this sudden escalation of rents…the linen industry collapsed as a result of a sudden drop in foreign demand. The cost of bread rose to famine levels, and the laboring population suffered severely."[179]

Benjamin Franklin had visited southern Ireland. He wrote to Thomas Cushing in 1772 that "the appearances of general extreme poverty among the lower people, are amazing: they live in wretched hovels of mud and straw, are clothed in rags, and subsist chiefly on potatoes. Our New England farmers of the poorest sort…are princes when compared to them.…The chief exports of Ireland seem to be pinched off the backs and out of the bellies of the miserable Inhabitants."[180] During this period, "Ulster was assumed to be better off than the Catholic west and south of Ireland—a land universally reported to be swarming with beggars, the peasant living so wretchedly in cabins no better than pigsties that the sight of them made the hearts of even the most frivolous travelers ache with pity."[181] It was recorded that many "families lived on potatoes and buttermilk in mud cabins and on a knife edge of threatened famine and fever as sanitary conditions were poor."[182]

What was to be done? The middling folk and the poor alike had the answer.

In 1773, the famed English writer Samuel Johnson toured Scotland with his friend and biographer James Boswell. Their days on the Isle of Skye were "very social and merry" and were often followed by dancing in the evening. One October night, the young people paired up and began the "common involutions and evolutions" of a Scottish country dance. Johnson then saw something new. A couple "whirls around in a circle," and then the next couple does the same, on to the last of the dancers, "till all are in motion....The dance seems intended to show how emigration catches, till a whole neighborhood is set afloat." What was the name of this local dance? The young people answered, "They call it *America*."[183]

5

HAPPY MEDIOCRITY

The emigrants jammed together on the *Faithful Steward* in the summer of 1785—the "passengers of respectability," the redemptioners and the indentured servants—represented diverse elements of Irish society, but they all had one thing in common: they had no problem switching their allegiance to the United States, a land inhabited by former rebels. Boswell considered their indifference to remaining British subjects to be "a mortal sign for the country."[184]

Among the English commentariat, there was anger, bewilderment and recrimination at war's end. An entire continent was lost to England, a virgin continent, largely unexplored and containing a wealth of natural resources that could hardly be guessed at. There was also fear. "Every inhabitant taken from us, and added to America, diminishes the strength of this country in a twofold ratio; not only as a simple loss, but as an acquisition to a foreign State, which may turn its arms against us, whenever interest or ambition holds out sufficient inducement."[185]

For the elites, the literal floating away of the valuable people who worked their lands and generated rent monies was the subject of much public and private conversation. There would be no working families of a similar quality left behind to fill the gap once they were gone, and when they did leave for America, they would not return. Government leaders encouraged landlords to be "kind and beneficent to those who live under them,"[186] and many restrictions on Irish commerce had been lifted by popular demand over a short period, pushed along by an American spirit of reform.[187] But the middling class did not care whether the elites had what it took to be "kind and beneficent." They had a bigger prize in view. They wanted what the Americans had.

Edmund Burke had seen it early on. The Americans did not have abstract notions of liberty. To them it was tactile and real; one was free, or one was not. "In this character of the Americans, a love of freedom is the predominating feature which marks and distinguishes the whole," he said. They would fiercely resist "the least attempt to wrest from them by force, or shuffle from them by chicane, what they think the only advantage worth living for."[188] In Ireland, the Presbyterian and the Catholic could not practice law. That was not the case in America, which was brimming with lawyers. They were, said Burke,

> *acute, inquisitive, dexterous, prompt in attack, ready in defence, full of resources. In other countries, the people, more simple, and of a less mercurial cast, judge of an ill principle in government only by an actual grievance; here they anticipate the evil, and judge of the pressure of the grievance by the badness of the principle. They augur misgovernment at a distance; and snuff the approach of tyranny in every tainted breeze.*[189]

Henry Adams would write of the early Republic that, apart from the evil of slavery, America

> *was sound and healthy in every part. Stripped for the hardest work, every muscle firm and elastic, every ounce of brain ready for use, and not a trace of superfluous flesh on his nervous and supple body, the American stood in the world a new order of man.….Not only were artificial barriers carefully removed, but in every influence that could appeal to ordinary ambition was applied. No brain or appetite active enough to be conscious of stimulants could fail to answer the intense incentive. Few human beings, however sluggish, could long resist the temptation to acquire power; and the elements of power were to be had in America almost for the asking. Reversing the old-world system, the American stimulant increased in energy as it reached the lowest and most ignorant class, dragging and whirling them upward as in the blast of a furnace. The penniless and homeless Scotch or Irish immigrant was caught and consumed by it; for every stroke of the axe and the hoe made him a capitalist, and made gentlemen of his children.*[190]

Irish villages were abandoned as residents emigrated to America. *Library of Congress.*

What kind of person would make a successful immigrant to the United States at the time the *Faithful Steward* set sail? There was plenty of helpful advice to be found; it usually started with admonitions about who should *not* immigrate. In 1784, while on his diplomatic mission at Passy,[191] Benjamin Franklin distributed copies of his essay, "Information for Those Who Would Remove to America," in which he explained that he wished to "prevent inconvenient, expensive and fruitless removals and voyages of improper persons" to America. The wrong kind of immigrant, said Franklin, would be one who believed Americans were rich but ignorant hayseeds who esteemed educated foreigners and would pay them handsome salaries to occupy public offices. "These are all wild imaginations," he wrote."[192]

Benjamin Rush later said something similar. In his 1790 "Information to Europeans Who Are Disposed to Migrate to the United States," he wrote, "Men of independent fortunes who can exist only in company, and who can converse only upon public amusements, should not think of settling in the United States." He added, "Literary men, who have no professional pursuits, will often languish in America, from the want of society. Our authors and scholars are generally men of business, and make their literary pursuits subservient to their interests. A lounger in book stores, breakfasting parties for the purpose of literary conversation, and long attic evenings, are as yet but little known in this country....Men, who are philosophers or poets, without other pursuits, had better end their days in an old country."[193]

The English businessman John King explained,

> *The government of America abounds with thoughtful and moderate men, inured to attentive industry, and to temperance; America has no kings, lords, and high-priests, whose devouring necessities might impel them to premature commercial adventures: in their present state of simplicity, the farmers are the people they want, and plain mechanics, for the works of necessity; their flourishing agriculture will yield a redundancy of heavy and rude superfluities, and the superabundant produce will teach the necessity of exportation; but all this will be done principally by her natives, and dreaming foreigners may be obliged to return to their own countries to exercise that dexterity and skill which was not wanted among a rustic and industrious people.*[194]

To "the dainty sons of England," King said, "I warn and apprize them, 'that they are not wanted in America; and if they go there, they will be disappointed, neglected, and perish.'"[195]

America, wrote Franklin, was a place where "a general happy mediocrity" prevailed, where "most people cultivate their own lands, or follow some handicraft or merchandise; very few rich enough to live idly upon their rents or incomes; or to pay the high prices given in Europe, for Painting, Statues, Architecture, and the other works of Art that are more curious than useful."[196] To Franklin, the arc of success in America looked something like this: "If [immigrants] are poor, they begin first as servants or journeymen; and if they are sober, industrious, and frugal, they soon become masters, establish themselves in business, marry, raise families, and become respectable Citizens."[197]

Writers on immigration agreed that most newcomers would take up farming. Why? There was, said Thomas Jefferson, "an immensity of land courting the industry of the husbandman,"[198] and the profits to be made in cultivation were greater than those an immigrant could make working a trade in town.[199] As Benjamin Rush put it, there was "no business more useful or profitable, than in agriculture."[200]

Franklin was probably aware that his dispassionate explanation of what awaited immigrants in America would set the hearts of common tenant farmers aflame. A "hundred acres of fertile soil full of wood may be obtained near the frontiers in many places, for eight or ten guineas, hearty young labouring men…may easily establish themselves there. A little money saved of the good wages they receive there while they work for others, enables them to buy the land and begin their plantation, in which they are assisted by the good will of their neighbours, and some credit. Multitudes of poor people from England, Ireland, Scotland, and Germany, have by this means in a few years become wealthy farmers, who in their own countries…could never have emerged from the mean condition wherein they were born."[201]

"The value of these farms," observed Benjamin Rush, "has often been doubled and even trebled, in a few years…so that a man with a moderate capital, may, in the course of fifteen years, become an opulent and independent freeholder."[202] A generation later, Thomas Mooney was far less restrained in his enthusiasm. "The American farmer, Patrick, never pays any *rent*. When he takes a farm he BUYS it forever.…Remember that, if you please, you can, as soon as you get into a regular employment, save the price of an acre and a half of the finest land in the world every week!"[203]

American leaders differed on the question of whether to encourage immigration to the shores of the United States. Patrick Henry argued passionately before lawmakers in Virginia that

> *you must have men; you cannot get along without them: those heavy forests of valuable timber under which your lands are groaning must be cleared away.…Your timber, sir, must be worked up into ships, to transport the productions of the soil from which it has been cleared.…Your great want, sir, is the want of men; and these you must have, and will have speedily, if you are wise. Do you ask how you are to get them? Open your doors, sir, and they will come in. The population of the Old World is full to overflowing; that population is ground, too, by the oppressions of the governments under which they live. Sir, they are already standing on tiptoe upon their native shores, and looking to your coasts with a wishful and longing eye.*[204]

Jefferson thought promoting immigration was a bad idea. Was it a good policy, he asked, "to produce rapid population by as great importation of foreigners as possible" when "natural propagation" would produce the same number of people in a single generation?[205] Jefferson was more concerned with national unity; he saw the principles undergirding the American experiment as a novelty,

> *a composition of the freest principles of the English constitution, with others derived from natural right and natural reason. To these nothing can be more opposed than the maxims of absolute monarchies. Yet from such we are to expect the greatest number of emigrants. They will bring with*

them the principles of the governments they leave.... These principles, with their language, they will transmit to their children. In proportion to their numbers, they will share with us the legislation. They will infuse into it their spirit, warp and bias its directions, and render it a heterogeneous, incoherent, distracted mass.[206]

Jefferson was particularly opposed to attracting migrants for the purpose of manufacturing finished goods. "[L]et our workshops remain in Europe," he argued, and keep at bay the "mobs of great cities" whose preoccupation with "manufactures and handicraft arts" to suit the changing tastes of customers promoted "subservience and venality." He wanted farmers.

Those who labor in the earth are the chosen people of God, if ever He had a chosen people, whose breasts He has made His peculiar deposit for substantial and genuine virtue. It is the focus in which he keeps alive that sacred fire, which otherwise might escape from the face of the earth. Corruption of morals in the mass of cultivators is a phenomenon of which no age nor nation has furnished an example.[207]

When the *Faithful Steward* set sail in the summer of 1785, the danger, tumult and privations of the Revolutionary War were already things of the past, receding from the memory of ordinary Americans with increasing speed. The old European ways, the monarchs with their countless minions, were suddenly and startlingly irrelevant to everyday life. The American habit of looking always forward, of being entirely self-contained and often plainly self-satisfied, was gaining hold.

But in the years to follow there would always be an immigrant to remind Americans of the world outside, of the old order they had left behind. One such immigrant was the Reverend Thomas Dunn. On October 21, 1794, Dunn made his way to the Middle Dutch Church on Nassau Street in New York City. The place had been a horror during the years of British occupation from 1776 to 1783, a jail that was the transit point or the end of the road for thousands of starved and bedraggled rebel prisoners, its floors "one caked mass of dead, dying, excrement and vermin."[208]

Reverend Dunn addressed a "numerous and respectable audience" assembled by the New York Society for the Information and Assistance of Persons Emigrating from Foreign Countries. He spoke of his Irish roots, as one who had "but narrowly escaped the fangs of the most cruel and relentless despotism" of English rule. Recalling the Israelites' exodus, he

LANDING FROM AN EMIGRANT SHIP.

Making it to port after months at sea was a relief for everyone aboard ship. *Library of Congress.*

traced the origins of migration to the United States, equating the "mischief and blood" of the pharaohs with that of George III and Parliament. Their plans had come to nothing, he said; and by mysterious means known only to God, something fine had risen from the ashes of their collective ambition: America, a place where impoverished émigrés could call themselves a free people and make all things new. Dunn concluded, saying,

> *Had I the power of creation, by one magic touch I would call up to your view those myriads and myriads of souls, yet unborn, who will successively occupy this soil, and who, 'tis probable, will be the envy and admiration of the whole earth; and who will bless you and bless the Almighty a thousand and a thousand times that they were born in a free land and who will bequeath their liberty to their children, and whose successors will hand down this sacred deposit, as their choicest treasure from father to son, to the most distant generations!*[209]

6

THE METEOR

Going into the fourth week of August, the *Faithful Steward* was nearing Nova Scotia. It was less than one thousand sea miles from Philadelphia. The North Atlantic remained calm.

Almost two thousand miles directly south of the ship, the inhabitants of the Leeward Islands in the Caribbean were experiencing unusually sultry weather. The peaks of neighboring islands seemed magnified in the atmosphere. This "looming" effect, as the sailors called it,[210] set everyone on edge; the well-remembered and "dreadful hurricane" of 1772 had been "preceded by threatenings very similar."[211] There was no telling when storms would arrive or how strong they might be. They were things of the air, things of "a flux and transitory nature," which is why many called such storms "meteors"[212] and the scientists who studied them "meteorologists."

On the evening of Wednesday, August 24, the sky appeared strange and seemed to lower across English Harbor on Antigua. British men-of-war were anchored there, including the twenty-eight-gun frigate *Boreas*, commanded by Captain Horatio Nelson. On this tour of duty, Nelson was "most woefully pinched by mosquitoes,"[213] battling loneliness and performing the unpopular work of enforcing an embargo against Yankee smugglers who snuck into port to unload cargo every time he sailed over the horizon.[214] He disliked the scrappy Americans and he disliked Antigua, which he called a "vile hole"[215] or an "infernal hole."[216] As for the coming storm, Nelson was comfortable knowing that English Harbor was one of the best hurricane refuges in the Caribbean and there was no panic in the British fleet. At ten o'clock,

Hurricanes in the Caribbean were a part of life. *Metropolitan Museum of Art.*

northeast winds began blowing across the harbor in the darkness, increasing in strength by the minute. The winds reached "truly terrific"[217] speeds by eleven o'clock and by midnight were at full strength and "very violent."[218]

Farther west, on St. Thomas and St. Croix, heavy rain arrived with gale-force winds around midnight.[219] There were dozens of vessels at anchor in Christiansted Harbor on St. Croix. Their mooring equipment was not equal to the force of the wind, and one by one their anchor lines parted, setting them adrift. Desperate crews struggled to lay out their heaviest ground tackle and best anchors to save themselves from driving ashore.[220]

The hurricane that arrived in the Caribbean on August 24 brought rain and damaging winds from St. Croix in the Windward Islands all the way down to Barbados, 470 miles to the southeast in the Leeward Islands.[221] Cape Verde storms born off the coast of Africa are powerful and have long lives.[222] They can wander for many days, nudged and pushed by steering winds and zones of high pressure, laying down a meandering track that looks like a careless doodle on a map. In the end, however, many hurricanes trend to the north, riding along the edge of the subtropical ridge of high pressure that dominates the Atlantic Ocean. This ridge pushes them close to the American shoreline. And it holds them close to the great energy source that keeps them both violent and alive, the warm waters of the Gulf Stream.

The hurricane blew out of Antigua on the morning of August 25. It was not as dangerous a storm as many feared. It had knocked down fences, carried away some tree limbs, damaged a number of crops and made an end of some small boats, "but nothing to throw us under deep dejection or woeful countenances," the papers would later report, adding that "some of our cabbage-headed prognosticators say the storm is not all over, but a Theban-Hall soothsayer says we may open our windows and sing Te-Deum."[223] Nelson summed it up for a friend, "We had a most severe gale of wind; the mischief is great, but not so much as might have been expected."[224]

The storm's mischief was far greater across the islands to the north and west, which found themselves in the right front quadrant of the storm, where wind speeds were faster. At St. Eustatius, four vessels were blown from their anchorages into the open ocean. They were never seen again.[225] On St. Barts, "An elegant house lately erected for the Swedish Governor was blown down, and a great deal of damage was done in the country."[226] At St. Croix, "36 sail of vessels at anchor were all driven on shore with the greatest precipitance.…Almost all the wooden houses and works in the country were levelled and the sugar plantations are so far ruined, that it is imagined they will not afford more than half their annual crop.…The whole loss upon the island, is computed at 3,000,000 pieces of eight."[227] Ships loaded with sugar and ready to sail were wrecked or sunk, with "a number of the best dwelling houses, boiling houses, and mills being overwhelmed in one promiscuous ruin."[228]

At seven o'clock in the evening of August 25, hurricane winds from the northeast began crossing the island of Puerto Rico. A sloop named *Endeavor* under a Captain Sample was lost with all hands,[229] and many other vessels were reported missing.[230] The hurricane then visited "inconceivable mischief" on "the sea-port towns on the north side of Hispaniola."[231] As the storm moved west, local trading vessels fled before the wind into the open waters of the Caribbean Sea.[232]

On Friday, August 26, the residents of Kingstown, Jamaica, were concerned by the "extremely sultry"[233] atmosphere that came over the town. Like the locals of Antigua two days before, they wondered if it was the prelude to a hurricane. The islanders were weary of storms: their "ill-fated country" had been visited by three of them "within the last five years,"[234] and they had hardly recovered from a "dreadful hurricane" that hit the island the previous July.[235] If anyone needed evidence of the power of that storm, they need only look at a schooner belonging to captain Gideon Duncan, which lay high, dry and derelict on the shore down by Fort Augusta, where it had floated in on the storm surge from Port Royal. Every effort to get it back into the water over the past year had failed.[236]

Veteran sailors studied "The Law of Storms" to avoid trouble. *Metropolitan Museum of Art.*

The wind gained speed as evening came on, "until ten o'clock, when the darkness of the night, the roaring of the winds and rain, and the general convulsion of the elements, exhibited the most striking picture of the deepest horror."[237] The wind raged "with inconceivable fury until five o'clock on Sunday morning."[238]

In Jamaica, the sun had "set on a landscape of the greatest beauty and fertility, and rose on the following morning over an utter desolation and waste. The prospect at daybreak…was that of January in Europe."[239] Dawn came with a heavy, driving rain; "every street in town was a roaring river, and every lane a rapid creek."[240] The waterfront was littered with wrecks. A whole menagerie of vessels had been caught up in the hurricane: the *Bull Dog*, the *Porcupine*, the *Swallow* and the *Swift*.[241] At least "31 brigs, ships, sloops and schooners" were sunk; the bodies of sailors whose vessels had been "dashed to pieces on the chain of rocky keys"[242] off Port Royal came washing ashore on the beaches and were "hastily interred in the strangers burying-place, immediately on their being found."[243] The storm carried away the desiccated remains of two pirates named Keating and Johnson who had been "suspended in chains to a lofty gibbet"[244] near Port Royal since their executions in December 1784.[245]

Captain Duncan's marooned schooner did not sink. It made an unmanned return to Port Royal, floated by the "extraordinary" tide across the harbor, where it was deposited atop someone's wharf.[246]

The destruction of numerous buildings across lower Jamaica offers a clue to wind speeds during the storm. Houses large and small, including those "fortified"[247] to withstand storms, were "unroofed…and some thrown down."[248] Free-standing walls were demolished.[249] In Spanish Town, "an inconceivable number of offices and out-houses [were] levelled with the ground."[250] One newspaper report said, "To instance the extreme power of the wind when the…storm was at the height, several stout cocoa-nut trees in this town, which had braved many a storm unhurt, were forcibly torn up by the roots, and others snapped off in the shaft, a few feet from the ground."[251] Sustained winds in a storm of this magnitude would be traveling somewhere between 130 and 156 miles an hour.[252]

The torrential rains blanketing the Jamaican hills collected in brown torrents of water that raced down creases in the hillsides, carrying leaves, branches and whole uprooted trees, drowned fowl and livestock, and the remains of broken buildings in a dizzying tumble to the seafront. The narrow, questing fins of reef sharks were everywhere in the confusion of the murky water, feasting on the spoils carried down to them on the flood. The hurricane, the latest of the "tremendous meteors"[253] that have forever haunted Jamaica, moved north and away.

In the early morning hours of Sunday, August 28, the hurricane made its way north into Cuba. The storm remained violent and large; it did "a great deal of damage" in the harbor at Havana. It sank four ships, "one at them richly laden from Lima," destroyed small craft of every description and broke ten trading vessels from their anchors and piled them up against the docks. Several islanders lost their lives as the wind tore the roofs from their homes.[254]

After passing the Florida Keys,[255] the hurricane spiraled away to the northeast and the open sea, well offshore but still making its presence felt through bands of rain, wind and heavy swells along the American coast.[256] It caused trouble at the port of Charleston, South Carolina. Captains there lost anchors left and right to big waves that rolled through in a strong gale of wind, and several coastal trading craft were run on shore.[257]

At some point, the storm's eastward movement was checked by the subtropical ridge of high pressure that dominates the Atlantic Ocean in summer, known to sailors as the Bermuda High.[258] The storm turned north around the outer rim of the High. Once free of its orbit, the storm came under the influence of the westerly jet streams and "recurved," leaving the East Coast somewhere off North Carolina and accelerating into the North Atlantic in the direction of the British Isles.

Whether the 1785 storm was as bad as the "the awful and destructive hurricane"[259] of 1772 varied from one island to another. It also varied from one person to another. For those unaccustomed to the experience of riding out a hurricane, it was the worst storm that one could imagine. A prime example was seventeen-year-old Alexander Hamilton, who was on St. Croix during the 1772 storm. He wrote to his father, "Good God! what horror and destruction—it's impossible for me to describe—or you to form any idea of it. It seemed as if a total dissolution of nature was taking place. The roaring of the sea and wind...the prodigious glare of almost perpetual lightning—the crash of the falling houses—and the ear-piercing shrieks of the distressed, were sufficient to strike astonishment into angels." Where, Hamilton asked, did a man's "boasted fortitude and resolution" go in such a moment? And of greater importance, where went one's trust in God?[260]

7

LOST

O n Wednesday, August 31, the *Faithful Steward* had been at sea for fifty-four days. At this point in the voyage and by his own reckoning, Captain Connelly McCausland had expected to raise the Delaware capes, but the Atlantic to his west showed the same empty curve of open ocean. The ship would have already crossed the eddies of the Gulf Stream, where mats of floating weed drifted north in the current. Beyond the stream, the water would have cooled and darkened with sediment from the rivers and tidal flats of the East Coast. Then, on a puff of wind, everyone on board would smell the good earth itself, the tang of the marshes and stands of loblolly pine. These signs would tell McCausland that the ship was closing with the American shore and that it was time to be ultracareful, to increase the number of sailors on watch and to throw the sounding lead more often to understand the depth of water below the ship as the seafloor slanted slowly up to the mainland.

Captain McCausland would have been on the lookout for a pilot to guide the ship into Delaware Bay and through the maze of sandbanks to the safety of Philadelphia. Pilots out of Lewes cruised off the Delaware Capes, going as far as fifty miles into the Atlantic[261] to meet up with inbound vessels. But the *Faithful Steward* failed to connect with one. Had a pilot located the ship, he would have been watching the sky cloud over and taken note of the long groundswell rising out of the south–southeast, where the horizon would be smudged with moist air and hard to read and the wind switching direction from west to east.[262] To an experienced pilot, these were warning signs that could not be ignored. The options rolling through his mind would have included driving the ship offshore to gain sea room to ride out the coming storm or putting into Delaware Bay as fast as the ship could be sailed to hide inside the giant curve of sand that was Cape Henlopen. Once there, he would set anchors into the mud, silt and sand of the Bay floor, scope out long anchor lines and hope for the best.

But there was no pilot. The *Faithful Steward* was, to put it simply, lost. "I cannot say whether the captain was much affected by the state of his reckoning or not," remembered James McEntire, but "the passengers and even the sailors began to display some uneasiness. As for myself, I became the subject of apprehension."[263]

Captain McCausland was a veteran sailor. He had crossed the Atlantic at least fifteen times. In the 1770s, he was almost constantly at sea in the command of two ships, the *Wallworth* and the *Jane*, running from Derry to Philadelphia and back, with forays to Cork, Lisbon, London, South Carolina and Rhode Island. This was McCausland's second return to America in command of the *Faithful Steward*. The previous summer, he had arrived in Philadelphia with a load of emigrants on August 31.[264] Given his time at sea, it must be wondered why McCausland chose sailing times that would put him on this piece of shoreline near the height of hurricane season. It could not be through an ignorance of tropical storms. Hurricanes were no secret to the ship captains operating between Derry and Philadelphia in the 1770s and 1780s. In the active years of McCausland's career, a dozen recorded tropical cyclones of varying intensity had troubled the coastal areas from North Carolina to New England, places that vessels engaged in the shuttle trade between Ireland and America were most likely to visit.

It is not possible to say with certainty why Captain McCausland delayed sailing from Derry until midsummer. He might have been holding out for additional passengers to fill his ship and make the trip more profitable. Or he may have intended to time his arrival in America to take on a lucrative cargo of flaxseed, which usually shipped from East Coast ports in the fall and was a mainstay of the linen industry in Ireland.[265] Or perhaps McCausland lingered in Derry because he was awaiting the arrival of a cargo of four hundred heavy little wooden kegs. He would have stored them carefully in the hold along the centerline of the ship and listed them on the cargo manifest as "Hard Ware" or "wrought copper." But that was not an accurate description of their contents. Each of the kegs was loaded to the brim with thousands of freshly minted halfpenny coins. And nearly every one of those coins was counterfeit.

8

RAP PENCE

On the morning of September 1, George Washington stepped out on the piazza at his Mount Vernon home to have a look at the weather. The wind was out of the east, scuffing the waters on the Potomac River and Piscataway Creek. Washington was hoping for rain, more rain. It had been a summer of severe drought. The intense heat had almost "annihilated" the Indian corn growing on his various farms along the Potomac.[266] The stream that supplied power to the wheel of his gristmill had run dry, and he was unable to grind wheat.[267]

In the middle of August, from his commanding view atop the hill at Mount Vernon, Washington had gazed wistfully as "a good deal of rain appeared to fall upon Patuxent and above us on this river but not enough fell here to wet a handkerchief."[268] On another day, it looked "very like for rain" in the morning, but the ensuing "light sprinkling [was] not enough to wet a man in his shirt."[269] Washington was later reduced to watching individual clouds; one offered "a pretty shower for about 15 or 20 minutes, but not sufficient to wet the ground more than an inch."[270]

Things improved in the last week of August, and the hard-packed earth began to soften up under regular and drenching rainfalls. The corn was "a good deal improved in its looks," he wrote, and the wheat "was up, and coming up, very well."[271]

Like other American leaders, Washington was a talented and prolific correspondent and spent a portion of his day writing to people high and low. On this day he addressed a letter to David Humphreys, a trusted younger

Washington could see for miles from the heights of his Mount Vernon estate. *Library of Congress.*

subordinate who spent time in the saddle with Washington in the perilous days of the Revolutionary War. Following his usual banter, Washington touched on a serious matter when he wrote that Congress was "deliberating on the establishment of a mint for the coinage of gold, silver and copper; but nothing final is yet resolved on respecting either."[272] It was a pressing issue: the country was so new that it did not yet have the capacity to make its own money. Washington felt that it was "indispensably necessary"[273] that the United States adopt a national currency. He had recently explained to a Congressional delegate that, without a standard American coinage and with so much adulterated foreign money in circulation, "a man must travel with a pair of money scales in his pocket, or run the risk of receiving gold at one fourth less by weight than it counts."[274] That was not much of an exaggeration. In his *Notes on the State of Virginia*, Thomas Jefferson studied the baffling variety of foreign coins that an American merchant might encounter on a given day. It took a set of printed tables to understand what a coin was worth relative to other coins in circulation. Making things worse, the value of a coin could vary from state to state. How had this been permitted to happen? "I am not able to say with certainty,"[275] Jefferson admitted.

Perhaps it happened because colonial Americans had not paid attention to their queen eighty years before. In 1704, from distant Windsor Castle,

Queen Anne issued a proclamation attempting to fix a rate of exchange for foreign coins in the British colonies. It was a massive inconvenience to have "the same Species of Foreign coins" valued differently "in Our several Colonies and Plantations in *America*," said Anne; it damaged trade and resulted in "the indirect Practice of Drawing the Money from one Plantation to another."[276] Using English money as her baseline, the queen went on to assign values to a dozen different kinds of coins issued from different mints in different countries at different times.

The queen and her assayers at the Royal Mint may have set out to clarify things but probably did little more than highlight the eccentricity of British money. Her explanations of how to convert foreign coin into British sounded something like this: "*Peru* Pieces of Eight, old Plate, Seventeen Peny-weight Twelve Grains Four Shillings and Five-pence, or thereabouts; *Cross Dollars*, Eighteen Peny-weight, Four Shillings and Four-pence Three Farthings."[277]

Queen Anne exhorted all of her officials "and all other Our good subjects within Our said Colonies and Plantations, to Observe and Obey Our Directions herein," or they would "Tender Our Displeasure."[278] It is not clear if anyone was paying attention.

The diversity of foreign coins in circulation in America not only made it difficult to understand their value but also made it far easier to pass counterfeit gold and silver coins. Counterfeiters or "coiners" were often tradesmen, such as engravers and button-makers.[279] They were clever people who could fake coins of any nation in any denomination. They could imitate "French and English guineas, and Spanish dollars and quarter dollars,"[280] gold "cob" doubloons from the mines in Spanish America,[281] "half and whole pistoles,"[282] English shillings and farthings,[283] French crowns,[284] Danish skillings, Brazilian Bahias and Spanish maravedis.

American newspapers were full of stories about counterfeit coins and often gave their readers detailed advice on how to spot them. In 1769, the *Pennsylvania Gazette* had warned the public of fake Spanish silver dollars "of a dirty white color, tinged with yellow; they are very little lighter than the true ones, the impression not so high or broad, the two globes between the pillars appear sunk, and the edge of an unequal thickness....They ring well, and are supposed to be a compound of copper and tin, lightly silvered over, which may be easily scraped off."[285] Readers in New Jersey in 1773 were told to be on the lookout for Portuguese Half Johannes coins, "something larger than the true ones, thicker in the middle than on the edge."[286] A close visual inspection might discover errors in lettering or something wrong with the king's nose or chin. Tests were suggested. "By dropping them with one

Counterfeiters at work. *New York Public Library*.

known to be good gold, on brick or stone, the difference of sound will prove them base metal."[287]

But many counterfeits were of a high quality. Phony gold "cob" doubloons from South America circulated in Charleston in 1773, but it was hard to tell them from the real thing, as they were "full weight, and look nearly as well as the good ones."[288] That same year, Bostonians were warned of Portuguese coins "finished in such a masterly manner, as to deceive, at first view, the nicest eye."[289]

Counterfeiting was an "atrocious crime."[290] The coiners themselves were "nefarious"[291] and "artful villains"[292] who operated in gangs. They were like something out of a book on pirates. One smooth-tongued accomplice of a coiner in Virginia named Low Jackson was "free of speech [and] much addicted to playing at billiards and gaming."[293] In Connecticut in 1785, some poorly made counterfeit Spanish dollars "were passed by one Jenck's, a man with one hand."[294] In 1771, another man fobbing off brass guineas as though they were gold was "fresh coloured, speaks lively and coarse, has black curled hair tied [and] talks much about jockeying and horse riding."[295] One who duped a little girl with some counterfeit dollars in 1767 was described as "a great drinker, and swears much when in liquor…is very complaisant in discourse, and apt to shew antick tricks."[296] When such people were caught, things did not go well with them. One counterfeiter in Newport, Rhode Island, was sentenced "to stand in the pillory one hour, to have both ears cropped, to be branded with a hot iron on each cheek, with the letter R," forever marking him as a rogue, and fined.[297] Others were simply hanged.

Strange as it seems, the most counterfeited coin circulating in America was neither gold nor silver. It was instead the lowly copper halfpenny, used as small change in everyday transactions. During the reign of George III, the Royal Mint in London was not coining enough halfpence to keep pace with public demand for the coin. As a result, "enormous quantities of counterfeit British halfpence [were] struck in Great Britain by private coiners."[298] These were referred to as "Birmingham Coppers." Fakes were also made in Ireland. In 1785, it was estimated that there were more than forty counterfeit dies at work in Dublin.[299] There, a base or counterfeit halfpenny was universally known as a "rap," a term affiliated with highwaymen or robbers in old Irish statutes.[300]

Counterfeit halfpence were "passed with impunity and indifference"[301] by most people in 1785. Why should they care? It was only a halfpenny, one of the lowest denomination coins in circulation. But rap pence had an undesirable and invasive effect on the economy. Even when the Royal Mint issued official, "regal" halfpennies, the amount of copper in the coin "was only about half the face value of the coin."[302] This was routine and a means for the Royal Mint to generate revenue. So, as the numismatic scholar Louis Jordan wrote, "small operation counterfeiters could potentially have made a profit even if they made full weight coins. Of course, counterfeiters did not make full weight coins, rather their products were generally from 20% to 50% lighter than regal issues."[303] They were not only underweight "but also debased. Most often lead, tin and/or zinc was used as alloys as they were more malleable than copper."[304] If enough of these trifling coins were put together, they might be exchanged for authentic gold and silver coins, which had actual value. Many feared that the public might hoard their gold and silver, taking it out of circulation, or that foreign merchants would demand payment for their goods in real money and carry it away overseas. If that happened, the greasy brown rap pence—like a kind of cockroach running around on the floor of the economy—would take over the money supply. Alexander Hamilton exhorted Congress in 1791 to pay immediate attention to copper coins, because "more valuable metals are daily giving place to base British half-pence, and no means are used to prevent the fraud." Copper coins might appear unimportant, he said, but they were a disease to the commercial fortunes of the United States.[305]

No one had explained this phenomenon with more passion and clarity than Irish satirist Jonathan Swift in 1724, who wrote a series of broadsides opposing the introduction of underweight coppers into Ireland by a politically connected Englishman named William Wood. To the shopkeepers, tradesmen, farmers and common people of Ireland Swift detailed "all the miseries that we shall undergo if we be so foolish and wicked as to take this CURSED COIN."[306] Americans remembered Swift's writings about Wood's halfpennies and thought that it applied to their own situation in 1785. The *Pennsylvania Gazette* reported that "the copper coinage, current in this city, is a reflection on the police, and must, in the end, be a general loss to the citizens, as the intrinsic value of most of the coppers in circulation is not worth half what they pass for. Scarce a British vessel arrives but what brings very considerable quantities of rap half-pence."[307] The *Charleston Evening Gazette* printed correspondence claiming, "Without the least exaggeration… there has not been less than 30,000£. worth (or supposed worth) of coppers imported into the United States since the peace!"[308]

Whatever the hazard to the economy, "there was a desperate need for copper coins for circulation in the United States in 1785," and a flood of English and Irish halfpence were arriving to meet the demand.[309] It was an illicit form of trade, and shippers attempted to disguise what it was that British ships were hauling into American ports. So, reported a committee of the New York Assembly in 1787, the coppers were "imported in casks, under the name of Hard Ware, or wrought copper."[310]

The *Faithful Steward* was carrying a large cargo of English and Irish counterfeit halfpennies from Derry to Philadelphia, some "400 barrels"[311] of coins being the most common estimate. Those "barrels" were likely small, sturdy kegs or casks weighing somewhere around seventy pounds apiece. The casks were man-portable and could be easily loaded and unloaded aboard vessels in river ports like Derry without the need for heavy lifting equipment. A typical coin keg would hold almost three thousand coppers, sized for easy sale to merchants or employers. If the estimates are correct, the

Faithful Steward was shipping well over one million coins in its hold, weighing around fourteen tons, perhaps the largest cargo of rap pence ever destined for the United States.

It is uncertain who owned all these casks of halfpennies. Whoever it was, they had connections in Ireland and perhaps England with the coiners or middlemen necessary to amass such a staggering weight of rap pence and get it all kegged and shipped to Derry for loading aboard the *Faithful Steward*. They probably knew the right people in Philadelphia too, with a network of distributors, merchants or other buyers who would purchase the coins well below face value and then use them to transact business.

The owner of the *Faithful Steward*'s hoard of counterfeit halfpennies would have to have been someone with no scruples about flooding the Philadelphia economy with underweight, debased coinage. That could have been one of the wealthy cabin passengers who were involved in two-way trade between Derry and Philadelphia. It could also have been the one man capable of holding the ship in Derry well past its advertised sailing date to acquire and load the tons of illicit cargo—the ship's captain, Connelly McCausland.

At Mount Vernon, Washington recorded in his diary on September 1 that "it began to drip slow rain" between nine and ten o'clock in the morning.[312] Within the next twenty-four hours, the temperature would fall and the wind would rise, increasing in speed from the northeast, blowing "pretty fresh" and speckling the windows of the mansion with a fine, "misling" rain that came in gusts.[313] In Virginia, on the lands bordering the Potomac River and Chesapeake Bay, a superfine rain and winds that rattle the windows facing the sunrise and the distant ocean can mean only one thing: a counter-rotating storm prowling the near-shore waters of the Atlantic.

9

PETTY AMPHIBIOUS TYRANTS

As Washington was making his way through his correspondence, the *Faithful Steward* was about 125 miles to his east, sailing in deteriorating weather off the coast of Delaware. Captain McCausland had been uncertain of the ship's position for at least twenty-four hours. The racing low gray clouds and heavy rains making up the outer bands of the hurricane would have prevented him from getting any kind of navigational fix from the sun or the night sky and limited his visibility to as little as 5 miles.

James McEntire had watched Captain McCausland interact with steerage passengers on the *Faithful Steward* over the course of the two-month voyage. "I must here observe," remembered McEntire, that the captain "was always respected by his acquaintances and those under his care. He was extremely kind and generous, to the sick especially."[314] McCausland had lived up to his advertised reputation as a "humane and civil" shipmaster,[315] caring for the needs of the families and individuals packed into the steerage space below the main deck. He would have been even more solicitous to his wealthier cabin passengers, who berthed at the stern of the ship and traveled in far greater comfort than the hundreds of emigrants housed in steerage.

That might account for what happened next. A cabin passenger by the name of Gregg, "having been married exactly a year, thought proper to commemorate the morn of his felicity by making a dinner to which he invited the captain, mates and a number of the passengers." Alcohol—perhaps a great deal of it—was served with dinner. McCausland, who did not appear to be a "habitual drinker" but rather "a very sober man," had more alcohol than he could handle, as did the first mate, Mr. Stanfield. "Music, dancing and every description of mirth succeeded," said McEntire. "A most intemperate carousal was the closing scene of the day. Among the intoxicated were the Captain and the first mate, who were borne insensible to their cabins."[316]

As evening came on, the *Faithful Steward*'s fortunes were narrowing by the hour. It was impelled toward a lee shore in rising winds and seas. That shoreline was low and made even more obscure by surf rushing the beach. The ship was probably enfolded in rain that came slantwise and hard on the wind. The light was going. It was late summer: the sun would set at 7:30 p.m., and it would be completely dark an hour later. There would be no moonlight; the little slice of a waning crescent would not rise until around 5:00 a.m. The Cape Henlopen lighthouse, built with such precision and at great expense, outfitted with new equipment and operated by the conscientious light keeper Abraham Hargis, was fifteen to twenty-five miles to the west of the ship's position, the spokes of its light blunted to nothing in the gloom of the storm. The Delaware Bay pilots had fled the scene; their cutters were snugged and tied off in the safety of Lewes Creek. And now the *Faithful Steward*'s captain and first mate were incapacitated by strong drink.

Some 875 miles to the southwest of the *Faithful Steward*'s location, Benjamin Franklin was working on his monograph "Maritime Observations," in which he ruminated on ship captains he had known. Franklin wrote, with his usual penetration,

> *It is not always in your power to make a choice in your captain, though much of your comfort in the passage may depend on his personal character, as you must for so long a time be confined to his company, and under his direction; if he be a sensible, sociable, good natured, obliging man, you will be so much the happier. Such there are; but if he happens to be otherwise, and is only skilful, careful, watchful and active in the conduct of his ship, excuse the rest, for these are the essentials.*[317]

There was no school in the eighteenth century for individuals to attend to become commercial shipmasters, no formal training that resulted in a certificate or license; the skills needed to command a large vessel were gained on the water, by observation and by doing. Professional sailors would explain that they chose to follow the sea "because they love it; because its bigness, its power, its ever-changing mood have a luring fascination for them," because they valued their independence, because "they will not be slaves" to some boss in some landlocked job.[318] What none of them would ever say was that they became sailors because they enjoyed ferrying emigrants from one port to another.

Emigrants were difficult. They were unseasoned travelers, noisy and needy. They were likely to complain. They got in the way of operating the ship. They could be a source of danger. They might be carrying disease like typhus, cholera or smallpox, and any one of them might carelessly start a fire that would be impossible to put out. Passengers caused sorrow: it was not uncommon for an elder or a child to succumb to some illness on the voyage and for the captain to be summoned to read the burial rite from the Book of Common Prayer as the body was left behind in the trackless wake of the ship, awaiting the day "when the sea shall give up her dead."[319] And regardless of how refined, attractive, bright or accomplished they might be as individuals in any other situation, a mass of people forced into the confined environment of steerage for weeks at a stretch was an unpleasant thing. One merchant who met an emigrant ship at the docks testified, "When we opened some of the hatchways under which the people were, the steam came up, and the smell was like the smell of pigs."[320] Shipmasters and crews looked forward to the day when they could offload their emigrants, fumigate the belowdecks by burning gunpowder or barrels of tar and get back to carrying nonhuman freight.[321]

If a shipmaster joined the trade to enjoy his independence or to admire the sea, he might not be temperamentally inclined to manage passengers. One captain responded to a delegation of complaining emigrants by having them "put in irons, lashed to the shrouds and flogged."[322] On another ship, emigrants were "cursed, abused, cuffed, and kicked" when they chose to air grievances about the food supply.[323] Thomas Mooney cautioned his cousin Patrick, "You must ever remember that the captain of a ship *during the voyage*, has more power over the crew and passengers, than any monarch of the Old World over his serfs; you must therefore obey the captain *while at sea*….remember, that if you raise your hand to a captain or his mate, while at sea, he may shoot, or stab, or cut you down, and no harm will come to him from the law."[324] Reporting on an abusive ship's crew in 1785, the *Pennsylvania Evening Herald* hoped "that an example will be made of these petty amphibious tyrants, who, to the disgrace of human nature, exert their authority in a situation and element where no redress can be obtained."[325]

Aside from Captain McCausland and Mr. Stanfield, the *Faithful Steward* was crewed by a second mate named Gwyn, a boatswain named William Linn and nine sailors.[326] As darkness fell on the evening of September 1, with McCausland and Stanfield passed out in their cabins, Mr. Gwyn was the only ship's officer on duty at the helm. There is no precise means of knowing how good a sailor Gwyn might have been; all one can say is that he maintained a westerly heading with the ship under sail into the night hours, unaware of where he was. And he was not taking frequent soundings, which would have told him that the ship was slipping past waters fifty-seven feet deep and then fifty feet deep and then forty-two feet deep and then thirty-four feet deep, with the bottom coming up fast.

As an English colony, and later as a state, Pennsylvania passed a variety of laws meant to ensure that shipowners and shipmasters gave proper treatment to emigrants in transit from Europe to the ports of Philadelphia and New Castle. The principal motive behind these laws was humanitarian, to "protect unwary emigrants, from the fraud and cupidity of unprincipled ship owners" who operated inferior vessels in the exacting and unforgiving environment of the North Atlantic and staffed those vessels with amateur crews who "were willing to brave all risks in the prospect of gain."[327] Rules that regulated the physical conditions aboard a ship, things like berth space, ventilation, medical care, sanitation and quality of food, were important to preserving the health of emigrants. But these rules were limited to commodities that were measurable and concrete. What they could not do—what no book of laws could ever do—was create the intangible thing, the "strong and skilled men" who would behave well in a crisis, "the men that passengers long for when the danger alarm clutches even the stoutest heart—for there has ever been danger at sea, and will be tomorrow, and then tomorrow."[328]

Maritime customs—ancient understandings and expectations about the way captains and crews should behave in emergencies—filled the void where written laws could not go. Among all the rules "never written down, but everywhere understood," it was expected that the captain would be the last man to leave the ship when it was in peril.[329] Why? Because his massive authority made him the single person most likely to maintain order and provide direction to his officers and crew, which was essential in the chaos of a maritime accident.

Many bad things could happen at sea. It was rather common for passenger ships to run aground on submerged sandbars near shore. A book on seamanship articulated very simply what should happen next: As boats were deployed to take the passengers off, "Any headlong rushing and crowding [to the boats] should be prevented, and the captain of the vessel should remain on board, to preserve order, until every other person has left. Women, children, helpless persons, and passengers should be passed into the boat first."[330]

There was no single defining feature among the standout ship captains who fulfilled every public expectation of how a leader ought to behave in a crisis. They could be very different beings. There were seasoned leaders like Commodore Edward Pellew, who could perform command and control miracles on the way to dinner. In 1796, Pellew and his wife, Susan, "were driving to a dinner party at Plymouth, when we saw crowds running to the Hoe, and learning it was a wreck I left the carriage to take her on, and joined the crowd." It was the East Indiaman *Dutton*, "crowded with troops and their families proceeding on the expedition to the West Indies [and] driven on the rocks under the citadel at Plymouth." The water was freezing and the forty-year-old Pellew was not dressed for a swim, but, he said:

> *I saw the loss of the whole five or six hundred was inevitable without someone to direct them, for the last officer was pulled on shore as I reached the surf. I urged their return, which was refused, upon which I made the rope fast to myself, and was hauled through the surf on board,—established order, and did not leave her until every soul was saved but the boatswain, who would not go before me. I got safe, and so did he, and the ship went all to pieces.*[331]

In contrast to Commodore Pellew, a skipper named Richard Sherman had very little in the way of credentials when he commanded the steamboat *Phoenix* on a night voyage across Lake Champlain in 1819. At about midnight, a

> *fire broke out…and soon raged with irresistible violence. The passengers roused by the alarm from their slumbers, and waking to a terrible sense of impending destruction, rushed in crowds upon the deck and attempted to seize the boats. Here, however, they were met by [Sherman], who… stood by the gangway of his vessel, with a pistol in each hand, determined to prevent any person from jumping into the boats before they were properly lowered into the water, and prepared to receive their living freight. With the utmost coolness and presence of mind he superintended the necessary preparations, and in a few minutes the boats were lowered away, and the passengers received safely on board.*

The boats gone, Sherman discovered a chambermaid passed out under a settee, lashed her to a plank and swam her to shore. Sherman was nineteen years old; he was only filling in for the true captain of the *Phoenix*, his father, Jahaziel, who was sick ashore with the flu.[332]

What no one wanted or expected from their captain was histrionics. In 1812, the highly polished Sandra Kollock Harris, wife of a prominent North Carolina judge, explained to her sister what happened when her ship went aground off Cape Hatteras.

> At about five o'clock in the morning of the 24th we struck. *Conceive, if you can, my dear Mary, the horrors of that moment! In an instant we were all out of our berths; the captain flew on deck, the vessel began to fill with water and inclined much on one side, which was soon overflown. Down the cabin stairs rushed the captain, exclaiming, "By the eternal God, we're on the breakers!"*

As it turned out, the ship was so close to shore that Mrs. Harris and her younger sister Lydia were eventually lowered out the stern window to rescuers standing on the beach.[333]

There was a hierarchy to who would survive a passenger wreck. If the crew tried "to save themselves rather than assisting the passengers," they had "a relative survival advantage" over everyone else aboard.[334] There were reasons for this. The crew thoroughly understood the ship; they were accustomed to working together; they knew how to deploy the very few boats available and so were often the first into them; and they were likely to perceive faster and with a greater understanding how dire the situation might be.[335] Time and time again, as newspapers tallied the hundreds of casualties following the loss of emigrant ships, their accounts would note that the entire crew had survived.

This was understood by experienced travelers like Thomas Mooney, who advised his cousin Patrick, "Never, if you can, be idle aboard the ship. Help the sailors to haul ropes, or to do any other work. This exercise will keep you *healthy*, and make *them* your friends; and you may possibly need their friendship before the voyage is over." Mooney also gave Patrick some pointers on what to do if things went bad:

> *Do not in strong gales of wind or cases of danger, which ships sometimes encounter, go about sighing, crying, or bellowing, causing the women to cry, which increases the confusion on board, and really increases the danger of all. Be cool in such scenes; pray from your heart to your God. Watch and wait: if the vessel founders and fills, there is little hope for the passengers;*

*if she loses her rudder, or her sails and some of her masts, she will yet float
about, and be relieved soon by some passing sail. If she is driven upon a
lee shore, and every one strives to be extricated from the wreck at once, then
many will perish; in such a moment as this you require the friendship of
some one of the active sailors, who may give you a trifling help or advantage
that may save your life.*[336]

Aside from crew members, single men were most likely to survive
a shipwreck. Their success on a sinking ship was "typically determined
by the ability to move fast through corridors and stairs [blocked by]
congestion, and debris," and by traits like "aggressiveness, competitiveness,
and swimming ability."[337] Women did not fare as well. Their likelihood
of survival was, "on average, only about half that of men."[338] Parents
traveling with children had a higher-than-average mortality rate, which
could not be credited to a lack of pugnacity or physical prowess; rather,
mothers and fathers simply refused to abandon their young on the ship to
save themselves.[339]

Captains and crews shipping emigrants to North America routinely
ignored the maritime norm of saving "women and children first." If sailors
thought their ship was going to sink, they often followed the more primitive
rule of "every man for himself" and looked after their own interests.

On the night of September 1, following the revelry of the Greggs'
anniversary party, the decks of the *Faithful Steward* were quiet and the "sailors
and passengers were mostly asleep." Second mate Gwyn remained at the
helm. When night fell, "there was not the smallest appearance of land,"[340]
but as the hours went by, had there been light in the atmosphere, light of
any kind, Gwyn would have seen the Delaware shore looming up in front
of the ship's bows, stretching to the north and south in a straight, narrow,
amber-green line.

At 10:00 p.m., Gwyn thought it would be a good idea to check the water
depth and directed one of the crew to throw the sounding lead. Pitching
the lead alongside the ship, the crewman would have been startled at how
quickly the sounding line went slack in his hands, the bottom was so close.
He counted off the tie marks and quickly showed them to Gwyn, who
exclaimed, "We are in four fathoms water!"[341]

Four fathoms—twenty-four feet of water—meant that the *Faithful
Steward*, which drafted between twelve and sixteen feet, was barely clearing
the bottom. In a panic, Gwyn spun the wheel to port to keep the ship's
bows out of the wind as he attempted to reverse course and get clear of the

shoaling water. This emergency "wearing" or "jibing" of the ship to the left was the path of least resistance in the strong northeasterly wind and pointed the ship in a southerly direction. It would be reported later that "every exertion was used to run the vessel off shore," which would have included Gwyn rousing out idle crew members to man the sails. But the *Faithful Steward* had little room for maneuver. The ship was no more than six hundred yards off the beach, with the wind and waves coming strong from the northeast, pressing it against a lee shore. The crew's efforts were too late, and "in a few minutes she struck the ground."[342]

10

THE VORACIOUS DEEP

In the days leading up to the *Faithful Steward*'s arrival off the coast of Delaware, hurricane swells from the south and east pushed water up the beaches well past the high-tide mark, creating a powerful hydraulic that pulled sand offshore and added bulk to the submerged shoals lying off the beach, bringing them closer to the surface.[343] It was one of these shoals, a long brown slab concealed in the turbid waters outside the mouth of Indian River Inlet, that trapped the ship.

In some strandings, passengers might feel "a gentle nudge" to tell "them that their ship was on a shoal."[344] That did not happen to the *Faithful Steward*. Instead, a sizable portion of the hull rose high atop a hurricane wave and then dropped vertically onto the submerged sand bar below. James McEntire remembered that the "shock was most tremendous"[345] as the ship's hundreds of tons of weight ground to a sudden halt in water fourteen to sixteen feet deep. Two children in steerage were instantly killed. Bunked together in the lowest tiers of sleeping berths, they were crushed by the weight of numerous adults sleeping above them when the cheaply constructed berths collapsed.

"The confusion that now reigned," said McEntire, was "inconceivable" and "beyond the power of description."[346] Most of the passengers in the dim spaces below decks had been asleep. With the violent impact of the ship striking the bottom, they were jolted awake to a world of noise; the "crashing of casks, tinware and dishes"; the clatter of "spoons, knives, broken bottles, basins and jugs"[347] spilling across the deck; the roar of the surf; and the low rumble of shifting cargo in the hold below their feet.

Fearing they would be trapped inside the ship, passengers rushed up the wide steps of the companionways or ship's ladders to the upper deck.[348] McEntire was among them. There was no ambient light for them to see their surroundings. If the passengers had been able to make out the beach, they would have seen an "interminable avenue of sand…and a low line of hummock and mounds, crowned with coarse grass…flooded in the darkness by a furious sea, which momentarily broke all over it, with prodigious uproar and confusion, reaching in places as far as the beach hills, and pouring through their clefts or sluice-ways."[349] "Meanwhile," said McEntire, "the wind had increased to a hurricane. The waves like mountains rolled over us, and threatened our entire destruction."[350]

The passengers and crew were soaked by spray and waves cresting the sides of the ship. The ocean temperature was seventy degrees.[351] At nearly thirty degrees below average body temperature, the water was cold enough to make some of them hyperventilate with the shock. The passengers were dressed for summer or for sleep, which meant that many were wearing linen,[352] a wicking fabric meant to keep one cool. If they stayed on the upper deck in the strong wind, the passengers would rapidly lose heat that their bodies could not replace, setting them up for primary hypothermia. That would contribute to their disorientation and confusion, slow their reaction times and make it more difficult for them to use their arms and legs.[353]

Of itself, early stage hypothermia would have challenged even those emigrants in peak physical shape, but the shivering, blue-lipped crowd huddling on the upper deck in the night hours had been at sea for fifty-five days. As country people, most were accustomed to physical labor and to walking wherever they needed to go; it was common for farmers to walk from eight to ten miles a day.[354] Living without aerobic exercise in the cramped spaces below decks and eating rationed, substandard food for nearly two months, they were in a measurably reduced athletic condition since the day they had boarded the *Faithful Steward* on July 9. The decline in their cardiovascular function would have affected their strength, endurance and speed.[355]

The physical disadvantages imposed on the passengers aboard the *Faithful Steward* in the moment of crisis were compounded by extreme mental and emotional stress. Today, when psychologists discuss disaster preparedness, they talk about the advantages of "stress inoculation," the idea that people can anticipate and manage their own reactions to disasters in order to "think more clearly," to "feel more in control and confident," and to avoid paralyzing "feelings of helplessness and futility [that] may cause people to do nothing" to save themselves.[356]

Stress inoculation, though, is possible only when potential victims understand the nature of the threat and have time to brace themselves for the coming experience. Nothing on earth could have prepared the passengers aboard the *Faithful Steward* for the disorientation that came with the violent grounding of the ship in the night. It left them stunned. It was a kind of ambush. James McEntire had carried with him "fearful forebodings of impending evil" since the outset of the voyage and watched with mounting anxiety over the last two days as one negative event tripped into another, the ship failing to make its expected landfall, the captain and first mate carried intoxicated to their cabins, the weather deteriorating.[357] These portents might have kept McEntire alert for trouble, but they would not have been much use to him or anyone else aboard the ship in developing a coping strategy.

Looking around at his fellow passengers, McEntire saw that some of the men "displayed much fortitude" but that others "appeared stupefied, as if resigned to despair, while others still, exhibited every sign of mental derangement."[358] These were common reactions in a shipwreck. Recalling her near-death experience on the Outer Banks in 1812, Sandra Kollock Harris noted the tendency among some passengers to remain hopeless and frozen, saying, "The gentlemen stood around like statues of despair, deeming all efforts to save themselves or us useless."[359] Commodore John Byron was a hardened veteran of the Royal Navy when he recalled the wreck of the *Wager*, a warship that went aground in 1740 with a complement of soldiers weakened by scurvy and seasickness. Even he was shocked. Among "all the various modes of horror" of that day was the sight of men who "became on this occasion as it were petrified and bereaved of all sense," who lay around the decks "like inanimate logs, and were bandied to and fro by the jerks and rolls of the ship, without exerting any efforts to help themselves."[360]

The great shadow hovering over the *Faithful Steward*, the dread at the forefront of every passenger's mind, especially those traveling with their children, was the prospect of drowning in the surf. They were not like Benjamin Franklin, whose love of the water and zeal for swimming seemed to his admiring contemporaries as nothing more than another manifestation of his sometimes-zany genius. Franklin saw it differently. To him, swimming remained a practical and important life skill, a means of avoiding the "slavish terror" of drowning. Now that slavish terror descended on the *Faithful*

Steward and "became universal among both the passengers and the sailors; for all expected the immediate ruin of the ship and consequently their own immersion in the voracious deep."[361]

The ship carried about one hundred women and children.[362] James McEntire's most painful memories of the wreck concerned them: "Oh! If you had seen that catastrophe from the beginning…the passengers rushing from place to place, while their cries pierced the heavens, parents embracing their children, and children entwining around parents…could you ever cease to remember? No! never, never."[363] The unforgettable noise above every other noise was the timeless plainchant of a shipwreck, the collective primal chorus of passengers fearing for their lives. "The shrieks and cries of the women and the cries of the children were insufferable," he said. "So dreadful were they that I felt, at times, a disposition to plunge into the sea, and thus escape the ceaseless and appalling sounds."[364]

In the modern era, carefully worded international standards for preserving life at sea place great emphasis on how passenger vessels are to prepare for emergencies, including the possibility of abandoning ship. These standards require crews to muster passengers for lifeboat drills and to ensure that "every person on board [is issued] a life-jacket of an approved type" and is wearing it properly.[365] No such rules existed for the *Faithful Steward* or any other merchant ship of the eighteenth century. There was no need for lifeboat drills because the ship did not have dedicated lifeboats; the mandate that passenger vessels carry rafts or boats to accommodate every soul on board was over 130 years away. There was no issuing of life jackets because the *Faithful Steward* did not carry those, either. It would be nearly 70 years before the first successful cork life jacket was produced in any quantity and introduced aboard commercial vessels.[366]

After striking the ground, the *Faithful Steward*'s crew may have waited several minutes to see whether the ship would be picked up by a large wave and pushed closer to the beach. They might also have adjusted the sails in an effort to force the ship across the sand bar. But the *Faithful Steward* had come down on the shoal with so much force and in water so shallow that it was stuck fast to the bottom and "immovable."[367] The situation went from bad to worse. The force of the east wind against the masts, tops, sails and rigging of the ship, combined with the pressure of hurricane swells striking the hull, began to turn the *Faithful Steward* to starboard, tilting its decks in the direction of the shore. As the masts leaned away from the center of gravity over the ship, they were reaching toward a point known to sailors as "the angle of vanishing stability," where the ship was likely to roll over. If the ship went "on her beam ends"—heeling so far over that the decks went vertical—it would shift the ballast and cargo to one side of the hull, submerge the masts and gunwales below the level of the sea and flood the interior of the ship. All of this could happen with astonishing speed.

In later reports on the loss of the *Faithful Steward*, newspapers in Philadelphia and London would record that "it was found necessary, as the last possible remedy, to cut away her masts."[368] This morsel of information concealed a world of desperate activity. To get at the rigging on the windward side of the ship, it was necessary for the crew to scale the pitching deck in the face of plunging waves that were boarding the *Faithful Steward* from the open ocean. Armed with hatchets and knives and buried in waves they could not see coming, the crew held on for their lives and hacked at the network of ropes, lanyards and shrouds that supported the masts and held them in place.[369] It is not clear who was directing the crew; it might have been a resuscitated Captain McCausland or one of the mates, or perhaps the boatswain William Linn, the petty officer who usually supervised the ship's crew when they worked on deck and who had "charge of all her rigging, ropes, cables, anchors."[370]

The principal goal of cutting away the masts was to ensure that the *Faithful Steward* stayed upright. But there were other benefits too. The masts, tops, trestles and crosstrees of a square-rigged ship were extremely heavy objects. Removing them would lighten the ship and allow it to float higher, perhaps pulling the hull free of the bottom so that it might drift out of the impact zone of hurricane waves and get closer to the beach. Beyond that, the upper works of the masts were still taking the wind, flexing, bowing and straining at the ropes of the standing rigging. Those lines would eventually break, and the unrestrained masts could begin to whipsaw back and forth, dropping tackle and spars to the deck fifty to one hundred feet below, trailing fast-moving ropes loaded with gear like blocks and deadeyes, which could swing like murderous pendulums across the deck.[371] If the masts were not disposed of in a controlled way, they could collapse into one another and fall onto the deck, wiping out the crew and anyone topside.

The pull of the masts on the weather shrouds was a godsend to the crew of the *Faithful Steward*. A couple of well-aimed strikes with an axe, and each humming, straining line parted with the sound of a gunshot. Then, with a jolt and a loud crack, the mainmast snapped about a dozen feet above the deck and plunged into the ocean, pulling the rigging with it and breaking off the foremast and mizzenmast, "all of which went overboard"[372] into the night.

Dawn arrived on the Delaware coast at six o'clock on September 2. "The morning came," said James McEntire, "but where was the prospect of our escape? It is true, we were able, when the waves permitted, to discern the shore, which was about a mile distant. But our ship was forced on its side, was immovable, and continually admitted water, and the foaming billows, which raged in defiance of human power, were between us and a place of safety."[373] Taking in the scene, McEntire believed that "there was neither chance nor hope"[374] that anyone would make it alive to shore.

To a landsman like McEntire, looking across the backs of large waves at the narrow line of the beach, obscured in spray and broken water, the shore may indeed have seemed a mile off. But it was an illusion. The beach was no more than 100 to 150 yards away.[375] The crew aboard the *Faithful Steward* knew this, and four sailors decided in the early morning hours to swim for it. One of the sailors was John Brown. The group intended "not merely to save themselves, but to raise the citizens and procure the long boat which had been cut down in the night, and immediately swept away by the violence of the sea, without having afforded the means of saving a life."[376]

The crewmen, said McEntire,

arrived on the beach, found the boat and fastened to it a number of ropes, which at the same time were attached to the vessel. The sailors had thus accomplished their part, and it now remained for us on board to perform ours. We, therefore, applied ourselves to the ropes, and succeeded with much exertion in drawing the boat within a few rods of the ship. There was the boat approaching, and here, in painful solicitude, were hundreds of persons who watched its progress through the stupendous waves. Still the boat was coming nearer and nearer, and still men, women and children were crowding to the side of the ship, each one contending to be among the first in escaping from the wreck.

When the long boat was only fifty feet away, the crowd gave "a cry that pierced the heavens, and seemed to hush for a while the roar of the vast ocean. The ropes had become untied or broke; the boat was dashed away, and hope itself was flown. No further attempt was made to recover the boat."[377]

McEntire was convinced that even if the passengers had succeeded in pulling the longboat into the sheltered lee side of the *Faithful Steward*, "we must have sunk it if we had obtained admission."[378] He was probably right, given the tendency of uncontrolled and panicked crowds to swamp or capsize lifeboats. Even if the boat were properly loaded with no more than a dozen people and equipped with oars, the return trip to the beach would have been perilous.

The veteran surfmen of the United States Life-Saving Service who later operated along this coast would complain of the "fatuity" of seamen who were "prone to at once lower a boat and endeavor to get ashore, immediately upon stranding."[379] It was, in their opinion, "extreme folly" to seek

> to make the shore in a boat, unless conducted by experienced surfmen. The appearance presented by breakers, when viewed from a point at sea, is so different from that afforded upon the land, and so deceptive, as to invite what seems a safe and easy enterprise, but one which is almost certain to result in disaster, not only from the treacherous illusion referred to, but from the ignorance, common among even the ablest seamen, of the difficult art, possessed only by professional experts, of handling a boat in the tumbling rollers of the surf.[380]

The attempt to retrieve the longboat was the only organized lifesaving effort made by the crew and passengers. There is no suggestion from any *Faithful Steward* account that Captain McCausland or any officer remained aboard the ship to improve the chances of the emigrants in steerage. The situation was bad, but under the direction of a determined leader, useful things might have been tried, such as improvising rafts from the planking, barrels and rope that lay in plentiful supply on the deck or awash in the lee of the ship. It is unclear precisely when McCausland departed for shore and how he got there. A Philadelphia newspaper implied that he and some others made it to the beach in one of the ship's boats, but the paper seemed to contradict itself a day later.

Regardless, McCausland did not observe the age-old rule that he must stay with the ship until everyone else had left it. With his absence, the other, older rule of "every man for himself" remained in effect as the *Faithful Steward* lay on its side in the surf off Indian River Inlet.

Ships die in different ways, some with a kind of tragic elegance and others with no dignity at all. A memorable comparison between ocean liners was made by an aging stoker named William Clark, who survived the sinking of both the *Titanic* in 1912 and the *Empress of Ireland* in 1914. "The *Titanic*," he said, "went down straight like a baby goes to sleep. The *Empress* rolled over like a hog in a ditch."[381]

The death of a wooden ship running ashore in a storm was different and distinctive for its violence. The loss of the fishing schooner *Red Wing* on the Delaware coast in an October gale in 1891 is a demonstration of what could happen to vessels that broached or pitchpoled in the surf. *Red Wing* was thirty-one years old and probably well past its prime when it struck a sand shoal off Indian River while skimming down the shoreline in strong westerly winds. It began to take on water. The crew steered toward the beach and climbed into the rigging to improve their chances of survival. The schooner then took a series of waves that flipped it over sideways or end over end. When surfmen from the Indian River Life-Saving Station encountered the remains of the *Red Wing* some three miles below the inlet, they found "a shapeless mass of spars, rigging, sails, and timbers, evidently the wreck of a small vessel bottom up, the sails and rigging being wrapped about the hull as though she had been rolled over and over through the surf and flung bottom up with all her belongings onto the shore."[382]

In the age of sail, the customary phrase used to describe the destruction of a ship aground in a storm was "She beat to pieces."[383] Sailors might also say "She thumped her bottom out,"[384] or "She bilged and broke up."[385] A ship could open like a flower, collapse in on itself like a riffled deck of cards or separate into two or three sections that floated off to meet their doom.[386]

Aground in shallow water and pinned to a shoal, the *Faithful Steward* was set up for a relentless battering by storm waves averaging somewhere between ten and fourteen feet high from trough to crest, with bigger waves arriving in sets.[387] The *Faithful Steward* would be a good-sized ship at 350 tons, but even a routine storm wave would dominate it: a cubic meter of seawater weighs more than a ton and a wave ten feet high and twenty feet long weighs about 410 tons.[388] In the near-shore environment, such a wave would move forward at speeds about as fast as a human being can sprint.

The dynamic energy of storm waves is not perfectly understood. Even now, research scientists remain puzzled at the strength of waves that appear "along high energy coastlines exposed to the open ocean."[389] The west coast of Ireland provides an interesting example. There, biscuit-shaped boulders weighing hundreds of tons and known as "clasts" are shuffled around by waves on cliffs well above the high tide mark. Researchers initially assumed that these giant stones could only have been moved by equally giant waves, perhaps by tsunamis or by superstorms. As it turns out, exotic waves are not the cause. Ordinary large waves produced by nondescript winter storms pack enough energy to do the job, not only pushing clasts well inland but also driving them *uphill* and sometimes through ancient stone walls bordering the cliffs.[390]

The more dangerous waves that attacked the *Faithful Steward* were smaller variants of the boulder-movers of the Irish coast, fast and percussive. As they struck the ship, they drove the caulking from between the planks of the hull, allowing water to intrude into the hold and lower decks. The pressure that the waves applied along the length of the hull was not evenly distributed, and this introduced torsion and flex from stem to stern, loosening the elegant and closely spaced ribs and frames where they met the keel. It is not clear whether the keel itself broke into sections when the *Faithful Steward* collided with the seafloor, but the ship's immobility suggests that it was. With a broken back, the ship might have been "hogging," its bows perched on the sandbar and stern drooping off into deeper water. By itself, this bending action would begin separating the interior structures of the ship from the more rigid hull, eventually "blowing up" the decks and dumping the ship's innards into the waters between the ship and the beach.[391]

The plunging waves coming aboard the ship scraped the deck clean of every raised structure and moveable object and made quick work of the lee bulwarks, the raised wall of planking that wrapped the deck. In fair weather, the passengers would have rested their elbows on them and watched the sea go by; now the bulwarks were jimmied loose or shattered under the tons of fast-moving seawater that mounted up behind them and washed overboard in the direction of the beach. Seawater also climbed the coamings around the hatchways and poured down into the interior spaces of the ship, soaking the berths and bedding and anyone who tried to seek shelter below.

The *Faithful Steward* was a well-built ship, new and supple. But neither it nor any other wooden ship was built to be held in place and simultaneously beaten by large waves. Ships at sea live on sufferance; no matter how strong, they are not equal to the power of the ocean. They must be permitted to bob, weave, recoil and avoid. Indeed, a whole science of avoidance would come into being in the years following the loss of the *Faithful Steward*, a "Law of Storms," to educate shipmasters on how to dodge large rotating systems like hurricanes. It would say, "The great point with the mariner is to avoid their fury, and, having ascertained their character and his relative position to the meteor, to make the best course for getting away from it."[392] The trick for the captain was understanding what quadrant of the hurricane the ship occupied and setting sail to slide around its violent core: "From simply knowing that the wind gyrates around a centre…we deduce the important fact, that, by placing a ship in a certain position, according to the direction of the *first* shift of wind experienced in a hurricane, she will be enabled to avoid, with great prospect of success, the centre of rotation, where the greatest danger is to be apprehended."[393]

The time for avoidance had, of course, passed for the *Faithful Steward*. The thought, deliberation and care that had gone into its making, the shipwright's quest for unity and strength, was fading away in the ceaseless crush of the surf. A hardened adventurer bound for Canada wrote about what it felt like to witness a similar punishment: "The storm was rushing and howling over us like legions of insane lions, or rather it was as though a Niagara of wind was dashing against us. The gusts seemed too solid for air; they came with the resistless weight of a torrent of water, bearing the poor ship down before its mighty onset till she looked like a helpless woman cowering beneath the rage of her drunken husband."[394] To Sandra Kollock Harris, the intimate first-person view of a ship's final struggle looked something like this:

> *We then sat in awful stupefaction awaiting death, but, O, my sister, it was death in such an awful form! I looked out at the door—naught could be seen but the awful breakers rolling over the remains of the vessel and smoking like a vast building in flames. The cabin was several feet deep in water, on which were floating trunks, baskets, mattresses and bedding. Crash! crash! went the broken vessel continually. The hold broke open with violence, and boxes, barrels, etc., were bursting out. The berth in which we sat began filling with water; the planks beneath our feet began to separate, displaying the roaring waves, which seemed gaping to swallow us.*[395]

In the morning hours, with the *Faithful Steward* breaking apart and no sign of rescue coming from shore, many panicked emigrants attempted to make it to the beach. Their timing was poor. The tide was going out. The tidal basins of Indian River and Rehoboth Bay now draining out of the inlet to the ocean occupied nearly thirty square miles of surface area[396] and were swollen with accumulated rain and water that had been pushed up into their tributaries by hurricane winds from the east. As this flood raced through the narrows of the inlet into the Atlantic, it intersected with a fast-moving coastal current running parallel to shore from the north. This lateral current fed struggling emigrants into the waters of the inlet, where they were carried away from land at speeds up to six feet per second, or nearly five miles an hour.

The combination of currents, one moving down and the other moving out, was comparable to a rip current, where a surplus of water that is banked up against the incline of the shore runs along the beach until it finds an exit channel and then "rips" offshore through the surf zone. Due to its "almost mechanical ability to exhaust swimmers," a rip current is known as "the

Powerful currents carried emigrants out to sea. *Wikimedia Commons*.

drowning machine."[397] The hydraulics at work off Indian River Inlet were on another, higher level. They created a drowning factory. James McEntire watched it happen to a young man named Campbell, a "polished youth and an early friend of mine."[398] As Campbell floated away from the wreck, McEntire "saw him carried into the sea by the reflux of water. I saw him at intervals on the liquid waste, far from the shore, far from the ship, far from the aid of man. Alone he contended for life, and alone he sank, to rise no more." McEntire looked on as "many essayed to swim ashore while the tide was ebbing, but every one perished."[399]

The water between the *Faithful Steward* and the beach was beginning to fill with wreckage. Everything that could float was there. Deck boards, hull planks and spars from the ship. Furniture from the cabins and steerage. Barrels, casks and boxes from the cargo hold. Chests, trunks and baskets carrying the passenger's personal effects, the clothing, books and tools they had packed carefully in Ireland for a new life in the United States. Many of these buoyant objects served as impromptu life preservers for emigrants attempting to reach the shore. But the debris field presented a major hazard to anyone entering the water. As the hurricane waves lifted, dumped and milled the contents of the ship in the shallows, they created a deadly obstacle course out of workaday cargo items and ship parts. Even when empty, an iron-hooped wooden barrel weighed over one hundred pounds. A deck plank of yellow pine measuring fourteen feet long and six inches wide weighed around eighty pounds. An emigrant paddling for shore did not stand a chance when such things were propelled down the lip of a breaking wave onto his head and shoulders.

It would be wrong to assume that everyone who perished aboard the *Faithful Steward* was a victim of drowning. Some were simply beaten to death by wreckage. That is evidently what happened to the men of the *Red Wing* who were lost on this same shore 106 years later. The Lifesaving Service reported,

> *The condition of the bodies of the crewmen when recovered from the surf leaves no room for doubt that they were killed before the last chance was afforded them to save themselves by swimming, one man being found with his neck broken, another with broken legs, and all more or less battered and bruised to an extent sufficient to lead the local State medical officer, who examined the corpses, to declare at the inquest that in his opinion death was not caused by drowning, but by the injuries received.*[400]

In the morning hours, James McEntire divided his time between the ship and the mainmast, which lay awash in a tangle of lines next to the *Faithful Steward*, pointing off in the direction of the beach. It was clearly a bad idea to swim for shore on the ebb tide; he watched as one person after another was carried out to sea. "Warned by the fate of others," he said, "I determined to remain by the ship until the period of the next flow."[401]

McEntire was not the only one waiting for the tide to change. Three men from a family nearby were holding on to the wreck "until the going-in tide" and discussing what they should do with their money. Like many others, they had converted their property into gold and silver coins before leaving Ireland.[402] They could not hope to stay afloat with their pockets full of coins, but it was better to have a little cash than none at all when they made it to shore. The men came up with a solution: they would each carry two or three gold guineas in their mouths during the swim. When the three of them crawled up the beach later that afternoon, they had taken such a pounding in the shore break that one of them arrived completely naked. It was not reported whether the men were able to hold on to their coins in the surf.[403]

The tide began to rise around two or three o'clock in the afternoon. Some passengers "went on shore by swimming," said James McEntire, "yet many were drowned in the attempt." McEntire was standing "on the prostrate mast watching those who were committing themselves to the mercy of the waves" when a cabin passenger "who was unable to swim, determined on going to land. He sunk, he rose; I seized him by the hair and saved him from the death which, in his madness, he seemed to court."[404] That cabin passenger was Samuel Hepburn Jr., who was accompanying his mother and sister to Philadelphia. The two women were carrying a "weight of gold which they had belted around their persons."[405] They were reluctant to leave their money behind, even though the money belts would make it much harder for them to stay afloat. They did not survive their trip to the beach. Samuel later "went to shore on a piece of the vessel" and lived.[406]

James McEntire's family—his father, mother, sisters and brother—remained aboard the *Faithful Steward* as it gradually disintegrated beneath them. With the tide moving in toward the beach in the late afternoon, his parents "urged my departure, and now to their entreaties their tears were added, as they declared it would be unreasonable and even sinful for them to require my stay, when I could effect my own preservation by going, and could avail them nothing by staying." After a long wait, hoping that the situation would somehow improve, McEntire came back along the mast to say goodbye to his family. His sisters and brother were weeping, and "in the bitterest anguish they clung around me," as his mother, "standing in water waist deep, tears flowing down her cheeks," told him, "Go, my son, go, and may God preserve you." McEntire made his way down the length of the mast but returned to his family, "as I thought I heard their screams above all others." He did this twice, but then it was time to leave. "Yes, I did go; but it was as the separation of soul and body. I swam, I rode upon the waves."[407]

As McEntire started his swim to shore, "The tumultuous waters were all around me, and the boundless ocean of eternity seemed to spread before my vision. The depth of the sea, however, was not very great, as I struck the bottom several times."[408]

Physicians in modern emergency rooms on the Delaware shore might nod in recognition of this last statement.[409] The waters here look deep when they are not, and large waves break in water no more than a couple of feet deep. Doctors are familiar with what happens to swimmers and surfers who make hard contact with the bottom in heavy surf. Each summer brings a fresh supply of new patients suffering from dislocated shoulders, head injuries, cervical injuries and broken necks. Injuries to the spinal

Few survived the swim to the beach. *New York Public Library.*

cord are of course the most serious. They can result from hyperextension, hyperflexion, rotational or compression injuries where the head is forced backward or forward, swiveled beyond its natural limits or jammed down onto the shoulders, fracturing the bones of the neck. Victims with spinal injuries may end up facedown in the water and unable to move, giving every appearance of being dead, their eyes rolled back and colorless. Even today, "once spinal cord damage is sustained, little can be done to medically repair it."[410]

No one on the beach that September afternoon in 1785 would know how to fix it, either.

McEntire remembered,

> *When I had nearly gained the shore my strength failed me. A sailor called Brown, one of the four who had swum to land in the morning, plunged in to my relief. I grasped him in such a way that he began to sink. He then tore himself away with an oath, exclaiming: "Will you drown us both?" He started directly for the shore, but when he turned and saw me struggling for existence with the odds against me he waded in as far as the water would permit, and so preserved my life.*[411]

James McEntire at last stood upon the shore of America, a place he had once imagined as "another paradise, a new and flowery land; such as mortals can never see, such as mortals can never enjoy."[412] He was about to learn that his newly adopted homeland, for all its promise and virtues, had a rough edge to it.

11

OUTLAWS AND VAGABONDS

J ames McEntire was exhausted by his swim to the beach and his near drowning in the surf. He spent some time stretched out on the sand, recovering his strength, and then set off to find out what had happened to his relatives and "to give my feeble aid to those who seemed to require it." The wreck of the *Faithful Steward* off Indian River Inlet had attracted the attention of the "country people" who lived near the beach. McEntire was surprised by the size of the crowd. "A great number of people had assembled along the shore; some relieving the half drowned and attending to the wants of the sufferers on the beach, doing everything, in fact, that humanity and an enlightened Christianity could suggest."[413]

The field of debris produced by the wreck stretched for miles along the beach. Among the jumbled piles of wet, shattered planks were hundreds of shapeless, pale bundles thrown up by the waves. These were the bodies of the dead. Some were dressed. Others had the clothing beaten from them as they tumbled through the shore break. In a "dreadful agony of suspense,"[414] McEntire picked his way through this open cemetery looking for his relatives and friends.

The human remains from a shipwreck were pitiable and doubly so when they were made up of emigrant families. Henry David Thoreau described them with an awful simplicity a generation later, writing:

> *I saw many marble feet and matted heads as the clothes were raised, and one livid, swollen, and mangled body of a drowned girl,—who probably had*

intended to go out to service in some American family,—to which some rags still adhered, with a string, half concealed by the flesh, about its swollen neck; the coiled-up wreck of a human hulk, gashed by the rocks or fishes, so that the bone and muscle were exposed, but quite bloodless,—merely red and white,—with wide-open and staring eyes, yet lusterless, dead-lights; or like the cabin windows of a stranded vessel, filled with sand.[415]

Many survivors coming ashore from the *Faithful Steward* were "miserably bruised" from contact with wreckage in the water or from the hammering they experienced in the heavy waves of the shore break. Others were seriously wounded and dying.[416] The people in the neighborhood of Indian River Inlet who traveled to the beach to assist the ship's passengers included a variety of laboring folk who probably had some level of skill in first aid.[417] Farmers, fishermen, sailors, foundry workers, sawyers and wood harvesters were accustomed to accidents and injuries. Many of them would have been familiar with techniques to control bleeding using tourniquets, lint, bandages and astringents like oak bark and the necessity of cleaning wounds and frequently changing dressings to avoid gangrene. They would have known how to reduce dislocated joints and how to use splints to immobilize broken bones. The country people would not have been able to assist passengers with more traumatic injuries but could have relieved their suffering with opium or laudanum, which was a common cure-all for pain. Mothers of every household commonly had a bottle or two of the stuff locked away with their arsenal of herbal remedies and medicines.[418]

Not everyone who came down to the beach had "active and benevolent" intentions. Some local people moved quickly and purposefully among the flotsam, debris and bodies at the high tide mark, salvaging everything of value. They were commonly known as "wreckers." McEntire was astonished when he saw them at work, "stripping the lifeless bodies of the clothing, snatching up everything of apparent value, heaping the plunder on wagons and hauling it away."[419] He recalled bitterly,

Many country people, on receiving intelligence of the shipwreck, hastened to the seashore fully prepared…not to aid in the cause of humanity…not to rescue their fellow beings from the ruthless waves, not to console the bereaved or administer to their wants. No, but solely to plunder till they could plunder no more. I even aggravate the case by stating that many looked with eyes of disappointment whenever they found a person both dead and naked, or alive and clothed; as, in either case, there was no hope of gain.[420]

If drowning could be described as a "miserable and humiliating" experience,[421] so too could the "fearful experience" of surviving a shipwreck. McEntire and his people had arrived on shore weakened and wet, penniless "strangers, in a strange land," "naked," "forlorn, and completely wretched," and were now exposed to vulturine "scene[s] which made humanity shudder."[422] Was *this* the "land of freedom, of civilization, of light and Christianity" that had filled McEntire's dreams?

McEntire's anger at the wreckers of the Delaware shore was shared by an unidentified subscriber to the *Pennsylvania Packet*, who had this story to tell in the weeks following the wreck: A girl traveling with her father found him dead on the beach. "After the first pangs of grief had subsided, she put her hand into his pocket, where she found a small sum of money; which she hoped would enable her to proceed to Philadelphia; but meeting with an inhabitant of the inhospitable western shore of Delaware, he, instead of administering comfort to the unfortunate girl, demanded her cash, stripped her father of his clothes; and walked off, seemingly callous to her lamentations."[423]

Questioning the ethics of coastal people who engaged in "wrecking" was nothing new. In the colonial era, governors on the Atlantic Seaboard had labeled wreckers "a set of indigent desperate outlaws and vagabonds"[424] or "evil and wickedly disposed persons."[425]

But the laboring folk and the "considerable number of poor people"[426] who lived on the Delaware countryside bordering the Indian River and Rehoboth Bays did not seem a particularly wanton band. They included "very attentive"[427] churchgoers with prolific families who attended services "in an old ruinous church in the forest"[428] and some who were fond of attending "frolics" or dance parties on the beach.[429] Writers in a later generation would note the "friendliness, sociability, curiosity, humor, self-respect, and general good will" of their descendants.[430] These coastal folk practiced a rugged sort of charity. They ordinarily tried to rescue unfortunates from a shipwreck, commiserate with the survivors, provide them sustenance and shelter and, when necessary, nurse them back to health. They also made efforts to ensure the dead were "picked up and decently buried,"[431] which was "very offensive" work sometimes carried out with a "great consumption of liquor."[432]

Despite its piratical and even ruthless side, there was no malice in wrecking. It was about seizing the moment. Every kind of valuable lying on the beach could be off and gone with the next high tide or damaged by the elements and made useless, benefiting no one at all. Ancient laws had forever recognized that finders were keepers and that people who went to the trouble and hazard of salvaging a ship or its cargo must be rewarded for their efforts. It was practical, and it was just. But the rules were also hazy and indistinct when applied to a particular case. When, precisely, did property ownership pass from one person to another in the hundred or so yards separating the *Faithful Steward* from the beach? A wrecker on the Delaware shore hurrying to load his cart with booty (even as his family might be tending to survivors) could say with a straight face that he had no idea whether this or that thing belonged to someone living or dead, but now that he had claimed it from the devouring ocean, it belonged to him and to his family. Lawyers might argue all day about the ambiguities of property ownership and the shadowy boundary between salvage and outright theft.[433] For the wrecker, the only thing that mattered was that he had possession and control of the loot on his cart, and that was all the jurisprudence that the moment required.

The takings from a shipwreck could improve the lives of a working family. Clothing was always a good find, whether it was socks, boots, dresses, jackets[434] or even "rich silks and other fineries."[435] The board lumber and timbers from a wreck could be used to build or expand a home.[436] There was a ready market along the coast for salvaged "masts, spars, deadeyes, blocks, shackles, stays, halyards, ship's wheels, chocks, cleats, and chainplates."[437]

Wrecking was profitable and exciting. *Wikimedia Commons*.

Vessels often shipped casks or bottles of alcoholic beverages that could be imbibed, traded or sold. Ships bound for Philadelphia, a place famous for its many taverns and townspeople, who were reputed to be "as liberal with wine as an apple-tree with fruit on a windy day," might carry rum, cider, punch, cherry bounce, Madeira, port or sherry.[438]

For shore folk, the little shower of wealth from a shipwreck seemed an act of divine providence. Some called it "God's grace."[439] And if the Almighty was somehow involved in determining when and where ships wrecked, then it could not be wrong to make a direct appeal to him. So, the famous old salvor's prayer went something like this: "We pray Thee, O Lord, not that wrecks should happen, but that if wrecks do happen, Thou wilt guide them [to our shores] for the benefit of the poor inhabitants."[440]

The further one moved away from the prosperity of the big port towns toward the "poor fishing stations and hardscrabble farms"[441] of the remote barrier islands, the more fervent such prayers became. The level of expertise increased too. Historian Paul Schneider wrote that on Cape Cod, "Professional wreckers had their rigs ready at all times in their barns, loaded down with crowbars, axes, knives, and anything else they might need to break open a ship. They paced the beach; they knew the propitious winds and the killer tides. They waited like spiders. The pros often worked at night, sometimes almost the very night of the wreck. They were very good at their jobs."[442]

This could also be said of wrecking: it was a positive thrill. "Most people, indeed, have only to experience for themselves the white heat of excitement which the circumstances of a wreck breeds," wrote historian Kenneth Hamilton Jenkin. "On such occasions, the most prosaic and respectable people will often reveal a predatory instinct of which they themselves were previously quite unconscious, and in the darkness of the night, with the sound of the breaking surf, and the singing of the gale in one's ears, old instincts and desires will awake to life again in a most surprising way."[443]

The country people flocking to the *Faithful Steward* accident site would have felt that "white heat of excitement" and that urge to compete. This was not an ordinary wreck, not some run-down merchant sloop hauling local farm produce or other "rude superfluities" like corn, lumber or salt from one coastal port to another. No, this was instead a wreck of historic proportions, the wreck of a lifetime, a ship full to overflowing with the personal property of wealthy strangers. It was simply irresistible.

In the late afternoon of September 2, as the sun fell and shadows lengthened among the dunes, James McEntire anxiously paced the beach,

The trauma of a shipwreck could haunt survivors for a lifetime. *Smithsonian American Art Museum.*

looking for family members. It was not until "twilight began to creep over the face of nature, and to conceal in its dusky hue the region of death and terror," that McEntire came across "an aged man, alive but insensible, and *he* was my father. I spoke to him, I raised him, and tried by all the means in my power to resuscitate the flames of life, and yet he still remained insensible and motionless." No one offered the McEntires any help, and the two of them lay on the sand as night came on. Large numbers of wreckers "continued to pass and repass along the shore," carrying lanterns that glowed like yellow orbs in the humid air of late summer. The screams and cries of terrified emigrants still trapped aboard the *Faithful Steward* came to the beach from the darkness offshore, a noise "terrific in the extreme."[444] There was no escaping the sound, and it made sleep impossible.

Some passengers made it ashore in the night hours. One of them was McEntire's sister Rebecca. "Adhering to a plank in company with another female she was discovered by two young passengers of her acquaintance who carried her to me," recalled McEntire. "It was a meeting of inexpressible joy, though I learned she had received many wounds by collision with the ship's timbers." James and Rebecca stayed with their father throughout that "long, long night," a "night of pain, of gloom, and of despair."[445]

The sun rose shortly before six o'clock in the morning. James's father remained unconscious and unresponsive. His coma may have resulted from oxygen deprivation from near drowning or prolonged hypothermia, but it is more likely he experienced blunt force trauma to the head, struck by a piece of flotsam or thrown by a plunging wave onto the packed sand of the beach, which was as hard as concrete.

McEntire left James Sr. and Rebecca to search for "the remains of my friends, and to see the full extent of the ruin." He was intrigued at the sight of the *Faithful Steward*. Overnight, the ship "had been impelled ashore" from its original position on the shoal off the beach. It appeared to McEntire that the interior of the ship had been scooped out by storm waves, but the hull itself remained mostly intact. Even now, as the hurricane sped away to the east and the swells diminished in its wake, sand was rapidly migrating back toward shore and filling the hull.[446]

The bodies of nearly three hundred men, women and children lay "scattered along the beach, as far as the eye could see." Only "sixty-two males, and seven females" had survived. All of the children aboard the ship were dead. McEntire witnessed many "fathers as they bent in sorrow and anguish over their offspring" and "husbands as they sought in vain for their lost companions." For all his searching, recalled McEntire, "I could never discover another one of my relatives except a little nephew, whom I buried in the sand." McEntire then "assisted in raising many bodies which were partly covered in the sand, and in burying a great number, of which we deposited between thirty and forty in one excavation."[447]

Astonishingly, the three McEntires—James, his father and sister—represented one of the largest family groups to survive the wreck. The Lee family had been annihilated. The beautiful Mary Lee was dead. James Lee lost his parents and five siblings, all of his aunts and uncles and twenty-nine of his cousins. Of the forty-eight members of his extended family, only six remained alive.[448] The Elliott family was almost totally destroyed; Simon and William survived but lost their father and five sisters.[449] In contrast, every member of the *Faithful Steward*'s thirteen-man crew had made it to the beach alive.[450]

On his beach walks, McEntire frequently came across a man named Gordon, who had journeyed nine miles from his home near Cape Henlopen with a horse-drawn wagon to do some wrecking. Among the items that Gordon had salvaged from the wreck was a chest "which bore the plain initials of my father's name," said McEntire. "I told [Gordon] that it was mine and enumerated its contents. He then broke it open and the contents were as stated. Yet, I believe when I was gone [Gordon] secured the box to himself, and I saw it no more."[451] The Elliott brothers also recognized numerous "chests and boxes containing valuable goods belonging to the family…washed ashore…but everything was taken by those bandits of the coast, the [brothers] not daring to claim anything and being glad to escape with their lives."[452]

After helping with the burials, James returned to his father and sister. His "father was yet insensible. Many believed him really dead." It was around this time that Captain McCausland made an appearance on the beach, "sound and well." It is not clear what role McCausland was now playing among the ruins of his former command; he may have been collecting the names of surviving passengers. When he came across the McEntire family, McCausland advised James to bury his father. "I felt inclined to follow his advice," remembered James, "but my sister would not consent. Her tears, her cries and entreaties prevailed over my partly formed resolution."[453]

McEntire sized up the situation. There were so many injured emigrants on the beach that his diminished family had not received "much attention, even from the most active and benevolent" of the country people. Said McEntire,

> *"I was exhausted, my sister, in consequence of her wounds, unable to walk, and my father in the cold arms of death, or in a state almost equally distressing to his children." McEntire decided that they needed a ride and so begged Gordon "time and again to remove us from the place. Whether through piety or importunity I cannot say, but finally he offered to carry my father and sister to his own house. Accordingly they were placed in his wagon and I walked. As we proceeded, I glanced my swimming eyes toward the place of my late fearful experience, to take a farewell view, when a conviction of my loss returned with such violence as to threaten a deprivation of my senses."*[454]

It took hours to traverse the sandy trails north in the direction of Gordon's home near Cape Henlopen. On the way, McEntire's father began coming out of his coma, showing "many signs of returning vigor"[455] as he lay in the wagon, with Rebecca trying to keep him comfortable during the jolting ride. Gordon told McEntire that he would only be able to put them up for a couple of days. This was unsurprising. The Gordons were not a wealthy family and, like many others living on the shore, saw a procession of shipwrecked and distressed people coming and going each year: they could not care for them all.[456] "When we arrived at Gordon's house," said McEntire, "we received some refreshments, having fasted about sixty hours."[457]

McEntire remembered,

On the following day, which was Sunday, my father became sensible. He had, however, no knowledge of the disaster. Neither would he believe, when my sister and I related the dreadful occurrence, that he had lost, and lost forever, the companion of his youth, a child of his love, or a friend of his esteem. He even insisted that we should return to the seacoast and bring all away. As we could not avoid it, we complied, and returned with many painful steps to the shore, which was eight or ten miles distant. We certainly had no hope of being able to recover the lost. And when he saw us come again, dejected and alone, he was easily convinced of the dreadful truth.[458]

From that point forward, McEntire's father was a changed man. "He never again, as I believe, attained that equanimity of mind which is essential to human happiness."[459]

On Monday, September 5, Gordon took the McEntires to Lewes, "where for some days," said McEntire,

we lived in the court house, as no one would admit us into his dwelling. While there I espied a man in the street, with a vest which had belonged to a member of my family. I instantly seized him and demanded my property. He refused to give it, and I insisted. The contest waxing fierce, two men, one of whom was a justice of the peace, observing us, approached and inquired the cause of the struggle. When I had explained it the justice commanded us to follow him into his office, and having under oath attested my claim, the fellow was ordered to strip, and accordingly resigned to me the most valuable part of his dress.[460]

After three days in Lewes, the McEntires were given "free passage in a boat to New Castle, from which place we proceeded on foot to Lancaster."[461] The walk took them over fifty miles of rutted farm and post roads, old Indian trails and portions of the "King's Highway" that stretched from Philadelphia to Lancaster. Despite its imposing title, the Highway was nothing more than a dirt road.[462] The McEntires then settled with a cousin who lived in Maytown.

On September 12, the ship *Congress* arrived in Philadelphia with five hundred emigrant passengers from Derry.[463] Thomas Lee and his family were aboard the ship. This branch of the Lee clan had planned to sail with their relatives on the *Faithful Steward*, but when they showed up in Derry in July, "the ship was so crowded they could not get passage and were compelled to wait for the next ship that sailed for Philadelphia."[464] When Thomas Lee disembarked from the *Congress*, he learned from survivors that Captain McCausland was drunk the night the *Faithful Steward* had driven ashore. Infuriated, Lee "armed himself and hunted some days for the captain to kill him, which he would have done had he found him, for he was a spirited Irishman, but the captain had fled from the country."[465]

Captain McCausland would certainly have traveled to Philadelphia after the wreck. He needed to find a boat to carry him home. He did not linger in Philadelphia. By December, McCausland was back in Ireland on his family's country estate at Streeve Hill and busy settling accounts with American flaxseed merchants in Rhode Island, whose paperwork he had lost in the wreck.[466]

On September 13, Dr. Benjamin Franklin made his own landfall off Cape Henlopen after forty-eight days at sea. Even as Franklin was saluted with cannon fire and pealing bells in Philadelphia,[467] typesetters at the presses of the *Pennsylvania Packet* were arranging a public appeal to run in the paper. It read,

> *In the most solemn, the most earnest manner, we beg leave to call the attention of the public, at least the humane, the compassionate, to the deplorable situation of those unhappy beings, the sad survivors of the loss of the* Faithful Steward*....Let us for a moment view the situation of these people. Just as they felicitated themselves on their arrival in the Canaan, this "land flowing with milk and honey," as their fond imagination pictured it, to behold their little property, letters of recommendation, their most indispensable necessaries, their wearing apparel, all, all lost; their nearest and dearest relatives torn from their arms, and swallowed up in a watery grave; some of themselves with legs and arms broken; all of them desolate and forlorn, not knowing which way to turn....Every man who is not a disgrace to human nature, will undoubtedly contribute his mite to alleviate their misery!*[468]

It was later reported by the *Londonderry Journal* that "the citizens of Philadelphia generously exerted themselves in succoring the survivors, and raised about 1000£. for their relief."[469] There is no account of how the relief fund was shared out among the thirteen crew, ten cabin passengers and forty-four steerage passengers known to have survived the wreck.[470] James McEntire and his family could certainly have benefited from the money, but they had already left the area a week prior on September 9, setting out on their sorrowful fifty-mile walk from New Castle to Lancaster, "houseless, homeless, penniless"[471] and still recovering from their injuries.

12

RED CLOVER

When the *Faithful Steward* wrecked in 1785, and James McEntire walked off into the Pennsylvania countryside with his father, James, and sister, Rebecca, there were about 3 million people living in the United States. In the decades that followed, the population increased by about 3 percent each year. By the War of 1812, there were an estimated 7.8 million people in the country. In 1831, the number was around 13 million.[472] Among this great influx of migrants to the United States, there was no particular reason why McEntire should have stood out or been remembered at all. But in 1831, a young schoolteacher named William McMichael was intrigued when he learned that McEntire had been a passenger aboard the *Faithful Steward*. McMichael wrote, "As no late account of that awful catastrophe [had], to my knowledge, appeared in print…I attended on him and procured [a] narrative, which I committed to paper."[473]

James McEntire may have been a reluctant storyteller, even as William McMichael waited with his pen poised to write it all down. The wreck was forty-six years in the past. Why, asked McEntire, would "I return to that scene of agony?"[474] Nevertheless, he did so, providing one of the most detailed and insightful shipwreck accounts of his generation. The narrative was a long one, around three thousand words, and McMichael would have labored hard to produce a clean copy of it while adding some editorial flourishes of his own. As an opponent of strong drink (he would later become a Presbyterian minister),[475] McMichael concluded, "Gentle reader, this dire calamity was, in a great measure, the consequence of drunkenness."[476] McMichael submitted the story to a local newspaper, the *Meadville Courier*. It was published on August 30, 1831.

In his narrative, McEntire explained that he suffered from powerful and intrusive flashbacks following the wreck. He said, "In the midst of my sorrow for the loss of dear and beloved friends, my mind continually reverted to past events. Both in my noonday reveries, and in my nightly dreams, I was oft affrighted by the sudden intervention of horrid images, and the scenes of the shipwreck were again and again presented to my view."[477]

McEntire's flashbacks or "re-experiences" were classic symptoms of what we now call post-traumatic stress disorder, or PTSD. The affliction is usually associated with military personnel who have seen combat, but PTSD is also common among disaster survivors. According to psychiatric professionals, there are nine distinct experiences that can initiate PTSD. McEntire had experienced eight of them. They included "life threatening danger or physical harm," especially harm to children; "exposure to gruesome death, bodily injury, or bodies"; extreme environmental violence or destruction; "extreme fatigue, weather exposure, hunger, or sleep deprivation"; and the loss of close relations.[478] McEntire's subconscious, ever sorting and ordering the routine experiences of his life, returned again and again to that deadly corner of the Delaware shore because it did not know what to do with the memory.

Other survivors of the *Faithful Steward* also endured long-term problems. McEntire said of his father, James, that, after the loss of his wife and children in the wreck, "his grief was great—too great for man. It was not a childish effusion, or the sorrow of a day. It was deep, interminable, and flowed with the flow of life."[479] The Elliott brothers, Simon and William, did their best to forget the day they had lost their five sisters and their father off Indian River Inlet; relatives recalled that "these men even after they had grown old could rarely be induced to talk about it."[480] Another survivor once visited with the Lee family years after the wreck. He "gave an account of the whole scene and how he felt after reaching the shore in a strange land, without friends and entirely nude, and there was a general crying scene in the family during the narrative."[481]

McEntire, his father and his sister, the "sole survivors of a once large and hopeful family,"[482] sought refuge with a relative in 1785. After recuperating, they found a home near Pittsburg. Rebecca got married. McEntire worked as a weaver and schoolteacher.[483] In time, he met and married a woman named Elizabeth Dixon. The couple had five children

An immigrant's life on the frontier often started with a log cabin. *Library of Congress.*

together.[484] Following her death in 1799, McEntire loaded his father and children and all their belongings on an oxcart and packhorses and headed out for the green, rolling hills of Crawford County, which was then considered "the wilds of the west."[485] When his father passed away, McEntire located a tract of farmland in East Fallowfield, where the family settled in December 1802.[486]

Around this time, McEntire married a younger woman named Mary Fletcher. They built a house on the new property and had three children together, two daughters and a son.[487] To support his large family, James set up a weaving shop and continued to teach school.[488] He "was a good English scholar, especially excelling in penmanship,"[489] and his teaching services were in demand in East Fallowfield and adjoining townships.[490] McEntire later taught at the "first schoolhouse within the limits" of East Fallowfield, "a log building erected in 1812 in the wilderness." There was an enormous rough fireplace on one end to warm the schoolhouse in winter, and the "firewood used was six or eight feet long."[491]

So, this was the place where James McEntire had arrived in life. It was not the America of his youthful dreams, "another paradise, a new and flowery land," where "genius expanded to full perfection; where every good was possessed."[492] It was perhaps more a place where he and countless other immigrants could create a life of "general happy mediocrity,"[493] as envisioned by Benjamin Franklin in his "Information for Those Who Would Remove to America." Franklin did not use the term *mediocrity* as a slur; it was the respectable, moderate middle, a condition that Noah Webster defined as one "most favorable to morals and happiness."[494] For McEntire, this translated into the freedom to support a large family on his own land and to follow his faith, free from the designs of an elite ruling class. For a man "who was so nearly as good as dead" on that summer afternoon when he stepped off the mast of the *Faithful Steward* to take his chances in the surf, his was an understated but obvious triumph. Within a century, his descendants would number in the hundreds.[495]

When McEntire gave his account to William McMichael in 1831, he was regarded by his neighbors as a plainspoken and moral man, a respected citizen not given to exaggeration or flights of fancy. Following their interview, McMichael commented that McEntire was "old, and must in the course of time, be called to the repose of the grave."[496] But like other disaster survivors, McEntire appears to have been made tougher and more stress resistant because of his experiences, and he grew older still.

Generations of immigrant children were educated in one-room schoolhouses. *Wikimedia Commons.*

Red clover, a forage crop and herbal medicine. *New York Public Library*.

It was twelve years later, in March 1843, with the ground beginning to soften and the threat of winter snows receding with every new day, that James McEntire sowed red clover seed on his farm. It was a popular crop for Pennsylvania farmers, who planted it by the hundreds of acres as forage for dairy cows and cattle. The flowering tops of the clover could be steeped to make a tea or pressed to make an extract said to be a miraculous herbal remedy that purified the blood, reduced joint pain, fought cancer and cleared the skin. When his planting was done, McEntire had supper and went off to bed. That night, he passed away in his sleep.[497]

13

MONEY BEACH

I n the years following the loss of the *Faithful Steward*, there was no icon like the Statue of Liberty at the entrance to Delaware Bay welcoming immigrants to the United States. There was instead the storm-battered lighthouse on Cape Henlopen, standing straight and white on its dune at land's end. Its steady glimmer was often the first solid thing passengers saw after months at sea, the first proof that there was something on the other side of the abyss.

In the meantime, the Great Dune on Cape Henlopen, over seventy feet high and two miles long, was making a migration of its own. It was best described by author John Rudolph Spears in 1890, who wrote,

Old observers do not remember just when, and do not know just why, this sand-dune became animate—began to roll inland. Whenever the wind was northerly its coarse sand was picked up in clouds and sent driving along with the gale. The light-house keeper or the beach comber, bound along the crest of the ridge, could continue his way only by covering his face with a thick veil, and even then his journey was painful. The cutting power of the blast was so great that new handkerchiefs used as veils during a walk of a mile or so were worn to shreds when the end was reached. The wind was picking up the sand from the northern face of the ridge, carrying it up over and beyond the crest, and then, because the eddies in the air could not sustain the load, the sand was dropped. Inch by inch the foot of the ridge on the north side receded from the beach; inch by inch the foot on the south side advanced toward the swampy forest. The ridge had become a wave that was literally rolling in from the sea.[498]

Reports from the superintendent of lighthouses back to the Treasury Department took on a desperate quality. Would the "big sand hill" drift so high it obstructed the tower?[499] Who could tell? In 1850, it was not the stone tower but the lightkeeper's wooden home that was most at risk. "The high sand hill to the north of the house, the base of which is but a few steps off, will soon be up to the house," the superintendent wrote, "and it will be but a few years before the house will be buried in sand, and no human being can hardly prevent it."[500]

It was sand that shaped a lightkeeper's existence, "sand that blew into food on the table; sand that ground into the window panes until they were clouded and dim; sand that was tracked into the house by entering feet; sand that had to be swept off the porch like drifted snow. On extremely windy days the keeper and his family were obliged to go in and out of their house by a window to save opening the door and letting drifts of sand enter."[501] It was only when the sand "banked up to the second-story windows"[502] of the house and it was easier for lightkeeper's children to roll out their bedroom windows than to take the stairs[503] that the place was finally abandoned and a new home built.

For decades, there was too much sand around the Cape Henlopen light; then came a day in the 1860s when there was too little. Moving "inflexibly in a certain course at a constant rate of speed for many years, presenting in its existence and movement a most singular natural phenomenon,"[504] the Great Dune was leaving the lighthouse behind and seemingly pulling the sea along behind it. Now the goal was "to prevent the sand around the buildings from being blown away,"[505] and by 1868, brushwood and bushy pine tops had been placed along the northern edge of the dune to stabilize it. But the erosion continued, as grain by grain, hundreds of tons of sand shifted "to the southward at the rate of 11 feet a year."[506]

Aside from the routine of placing defensive lines of brush around the site, serious and expensive efforts were made by the federal government to preserve the light. In 1914, construction started on a seven-hundred-foot timber bulkhead northeast of the tower, supplemented by four long timber groins with pilings twelve feet deep.[507] Like everything else, it proved a temporary fix. By 1920, it had become obvious to officials in Washington that it was not economically possible to hold on to the lighthouse complex.[508]

In 1924, to the sorrow of those living around Lewes, the light went dark for the final time, "discontinued because of erosion of the shore line."[509]

On the afternoon of April 13, 1926, the Cape Henlopen lighthouse fell into the sea. No one was surprised. The gyres of ocean current and unending sinews of wind around the cape, as baffling as they were strong, always had the last say. For some time, the east end of the lightkeeper's house—a rather nice-looking building with four chimneys and a porch—had projected out in space above the beach, with the very foundation of the lighthouse exposed and visible from the water's edge.

It was a clear day when the lighthouse fell, the wind out of the northeast and temperatures mild.[510] Journalist Judith Roales wrote, "The lighthouse simply lost her balance and toppled over," the massive walls of the tower's base lying sideways atop a field of rubble that spread down the slope of the dune to the beach. On the following day, in keeping with the long traditions of the shore, "scavengers and souvenir hunters arrived. Stones, brass and hardware were carried away by the cartloads. What was left behind by man was claimed by the hungry sea. By midsummer 1926, everything on the beach was gone."[511]

The wreck of the *Faithful Steward* off Indian River Inlet in September 1785 was the first mass casualty event in the United States. Some 290 people drowned or died from their injuries, about 80 percent of those aboard the ship. Yet there was nothing to hold the event in the national conscience. No monument to mark the spot where the ship went down, no great writer's essay or poem to keep her memory alive. James McEntire's narrative of the wreck, as fine as it was, arrived almost fifty years later. His story remained in relative obscurity, appearing only twice in small local newspapers in Pennsylvania in 1831 and 1881. It would have been natural, then, for the *Faithful Steward* to melt into the past, another sad parable from the age of sail on a coast littered with shipwrecks.

But there was a surprise in store down on the inlet, 150 years in the making. As at Cape Henlopen, it involved human attempts to control the movement of sand. While efforts to save the lighthouse had played out like a tragedy in slow motion, the struggle to control sand down at Indian River Inlet had a different feel to it. It was more like a war, complete with dynamite, explosions and men with shovels energetically digging trenches.

Indian River Inlet had served for centuries as "the heart-valve of the 150 or 200 square miles of the Rehoboth Bay–Indian River region."[512] But the federal government's construction of inland canals through the region's back-bays in the late 1800s reduced the velocity and volume of water passing through the inlet,[513] making it vulnerable to closure by large storms or littoral drift, the ordinary flow of sand northward along the Atlantic beaches.[514]

When the inlet sanded over, the water held up in Indian River and Rehoboth Bay could usually be counted on to punch a new channel through to the ocean. Sometimes, though, the inlet dammed over completely and stayed that way, which meant that the back bays were no longer "subject to lunar tides,"[515] creating "stagnant, mosquito-breeding waters on marshes and low shores."[516] A further complication was that the inlet was prone to move. It had "shifted in location over a 2-miles length of beach"[517] at least five times since the 1800s. And it had the habit of assuming odd and interesting new shapes, the channel kinking and curving around sand shoals that barred the way to the open ocean. One big shoal that emerged in 1880 was so dominating and challenging to navigators that the locals gave it a name: "the Bulkhead."[518]

It was an open question as to who was responsible for maintaining Indian River Inlet. When the inlet clogged, which happened with exasperating frequency, state and local officials would call on the U.S. Army Corps of Engineers to reopen the channel. "They claim," wrote Brigadier General G.B. Pillsbury of the Corps, "that deterioration of the original inlet was due largely to the construction by the United States of the two small canals entering the bays from the north and south, and consider its restoration a moral obligation of the Federal Government."[519] Whatever the merits of this "old and sincere local feeling," said a Corps engineering report, it needed to be remembered that the "canals were apparently constructed with the full approval of local interests at that time."[520]

The Army Corps of Engineers pondered Indian River Inlet for decades, issuing "preliminary examinations," studies and reports with desultory titles such as "The Problem of Keeping Indian River Inlet Open."[521] An admiring member of Congress once described the corps as "a disinterested body of men, highly trained, skilled and expert, with the welfare of the American people as their only consideration."[522] As unemotional guardians of the federal treasury, Corps engineers were leery of expensive "pork" projects that benefited politically connected cliques or tiny segments of the population. They knew that there were few things as costly—and eternal—as dredging operations. So, the engineers waffled and talked among themselves. Through the years, they repeatedly "expressed the opinion that no improvement of the waterway…at the expense of the United States was justified at that time."[523]

For locals in the tiny towns and hamlets along Rehoboth Bay and Indian River, the lack of an open channel to the Atlantic was a disaster. They considered fresh seafood a birthright. Harvests of crabs, oysters, herring, shad, perch, croaker, spot, drum, flounder, striped bass and bluefish not only put good food on the table but also were a way of marking the seasons, part of the rhythm of coastal life that gave it spice. In springtime, an entire village would partake in the excitement of netting vast schools of spawning herring by lantern light. In summer, a bushel of steamed blue crabs was a feast and social event rolled into one. In autumn, an angler hauling a trophy striper from the water felt positively wealthy, knowing the meat from a twenty-five-pound fish would feed two families. When the inlet sanded over, all of this came under threat.

As officials ruminated over a solution for Indian River Inlet, locals took matters into their own hands. On at least two occasions in the early 1900s, hundreds of unpaid volunteers descended on the inlet with shovels to clear a trench and get the water flowing again. It was slow and backbreaking work. They finally resorted to using explosives. A whopping 2,200 pounds of dynamite were once used to clear thirty yards of beach separating the river and the ocean. Yellowed archival photographs show the precise moment of detonation, a jet of sand rising one hundred feet into the air and blotting out the horizon; a picture taken minutes later shows a large crowd curiously peering down into the crater as water began to flow from the river to the sea. That new inlet lasted less than a week.[524]

In 1931, the State Highway Commission decided to build an "Ocean Highway" from Rehoboth Beach to Bethany Beach, thirteen miles south and below Indian River Inlet. The highway was completed in 1933, with a modest wooden bridge crossing the inlet.[525] The commission dredged a passage for two years and sank pilings to hold the channel in position,[526] but it was more than obvious that a significant hardening of the inlet was needed.

In February 1935, a Congressional committee directed the Corps of Engineers to study, once again, whether improvements should be made to the inlet.[527] The chief of engineers responded to the committee in July 1937 with thirty-six pages of reports and recommendations. Buried deep inside the document was a tipoff that the Corps was feeling some political pressure to approve the project, the district engineer noting, "Of recent years, the recognition of Rehoboth as a resort, favored by Washington residents, including both American and foreign diplomatic personnel, has revived the importance of yachting channels as well as the old hope of restoring the sea-food industry."[528]

But the Corps was at last ready to fold its hand. If Delaware would provide $160,000 in funding, build a better bridge and perform some administrative tasks, the Corps would dredge a channel well into Indian

River and construct "parallel stone jetties with steel sheet pile cores 500 feet apart and extending seaward approximately 1,500 feet to the 14-foot depth curve."[529] The project was eventually approved.[530]

On February 22, 1937, a company of young men employed by the Civilian Conservation Corps (CCC) boarded their work trucks in Lewes and rode down to Indian River Inlet. During the Depression, CCC workers in southern Delaware were tasked with digging drainage channels across marshlands to control mosquitoes and constructing wooden bulwarks to keep shorefront properties from washing away.[531] The young CCC men might have been there on that Monday morning to dig canals in Rehoboth Bay or to reinforce the dunes along Ocean Highway, which was prone to over-wash during storms. Whatever the reason, they made their way down to the beach and were astonished to find the shorefront by the inlet littered with hundreds of copper coins.

Bronze or green in color and lightly frosted with sand, the halfpenny coins were worn from years in the sea. The obverse sides of the coins read "GEORGIVS III REX" and portrayed the king wearing laurels around his head. On some coins, the reverse featured "BRITANNIA," a robed lady sitting atop a globe, her right hand extending an olive branch and her left hand holding a staff, by her side a shield bearing the crosses of Saints George and Andrew. These were "English" halfpennies. The remaining coins were "Irish" halfpennies, each showing a harp beneath a crown under the legend "HIBERNIA," the Latin name for Ireland.

The next day, the *New York Times* reported that the CCC workers had found "several hundred" halfpennies dating between 1774 and 1782 and that "a holiday treasure hunt revealed more."[532] This was one of the first reported hoards of coppers recovered from the wreck site of the *Faithful Steward*.

Over the years, a variety of old coins had been picked up by fisherman, beachcombers and surfmen on the shore above Indian River Inlet following strong northeasterly storms.[533] But the sudden appearance of hundreds of coins on the beach was something new. How did it happen? The most likely explanation was that one of the dredges used to keep the mouth of the inlet open by moving sand from the seafloor to the beach had cut across the remains of the *Faithful Steward*. Even after 150 years, the ship's heavy keel and ribs could have been lying intact on the peat and clay of the primordial forest floor, concealed deep in the darkness below hundreds of tons of sediment and sand. Its heaviest cargo would be there, too, dense kegs of halfpennies clustered along the length of the keel, between the frames, or resting in a scatter pattern close to the wreck.

A hydraulic dredge would have made short work of all this. The rotating steel head on a cutter suction-dredge was built so tough and spun so fast that it could break rock.[534] As the dredge burrowed into the sea bottom, debris would be vacuumed up a pipe and sprayed onto the beach, a dirty fountain of water, sand, gray clay, chunks of brown peat and broken shells, with coins in the mix. Some coins would be cupped or bent at the edges, mutilated by the head of the dredge or damaged as they sped through the pipe to the surface. Other coins, freed from their broken kegs, would have spread across the ocean floor to begin a slow journey through the surf zone to the beach, moved by big storm waves of the kind that had destroyed the ship. Most of those eventually flipped up to the high-tide mark, where they were sometimes found lying in perfect rows as though arranged on a surveyor's transit line.

In the weeks and months that followed, "hundreds of treasure seekers from near-by States"[535] and "collectors from far parts of the country"[536] descended on what was coming to be known as "Coin Beach." It was reported that beachcombers occasionally found gold and silver coins during their hunts "on the beach or back among the dunes."[537] These finds were certainly more exciting than halfpennies, but they were comparatively rare. There were not enough of them to suggest that the *Faithful Steward* was carrying a cargo of treasure coins. Perhaps these were the contents of Captain McCausland's strongbox, left behind in his hurry to abandon ship. But gold guineas and silver shillings were more likely the personal property of the emigrants themselves. Thomas Mooney had written, "I have often been asked what is the best thing for an emigrant to bring out…[to] the New World. I answer, *ready money*."[538] This was the shared opinion of the Irish in the eighteenth and nineteenth centuries. A crowded emigrant ship from the British Isles could be carrying many thousands of pieces of gold, the life savings of those aboard, intended for the start of a new life in America.[539]

In the summer of 1938, the hydraulic dredge *Margate* got to work at Indian River Inlet, clearing a channel fifteen feet deep.[540] On September 13, the engineers working the dredge came across the remains of a wooden wreck "and some ancient coins apparently minted in Ireland and bearing dates of 1781 and 1772. Dredging was suspended and a treasure hunt was on."[541] Government inspectors assumed these were the remains of the *Faithful Steward*.[542] Locals apparently wanted to salvage more coins, but a series of storms hit the coast in the days following the discovery, removing the overburden of mud and sand from the wreckage. The ship's remains refloated on the storm surge and were carried out to sea.[543]

Beachcombing is a relaxing tradition on the Mid-Atlantic coast. *Library of Congress.*

The *Faithful Steward* proved to be a generous and reliable source of halfpennies in the years following the improvement of Indian River Inlet. On news that a hurricane or northeaster had blown through, people would travel from hundreds of miles away to search for them.[544] This was in keeping with the coastal lifestyle: if coins were being found on the beaches of Fenwick Island, everyone stopped what they were doing and headed for the shore. As far back as 1857, the *New York Times* had reported, "The excitement among the natives is said to be great. Crops are left untilled, shops and stores are closed, and thousands of persons are on the beach raking for silver."[545]

Coin hunts were far easier for vacationers and residents from nearby resorts, who could drive to Indian River Inlet in a matter of minutes on the new Ocean Highway. Some said that children gathered "pails of British and Irish half-pennies" that were as "numerous as clam shells."[546] Wealthy older women from Philadelphia, summering in their cottages beneath the stands of loblolly pines in Rehoboth Beach, got in on the action too.

The *New York Times* reported on September 1, 1939:

> *Beach combing for coppers has turned the thoughts of Summer visitors here from the foreign situation. Daybreak yesterday found scores of persons at this resort's "money beach" five miles south of the ocean front near the Indian*

River inlet in search of copper pieces, minted nearly two centuries ago in the reigns of King George II and III of England. Salvaging was excellent after six days of a northeasterly blow and pounding seas. Nearly 500 were located. Dates were from 1725 to 1780. Two Philadelphia matrons on Monday found nineteen coins. Mrs. Harry Fehr of Whitemarsh located thirty-nine, while her sister, Mrs. John W. Watson of Chestnut Hill, added forty-four. The coins, believed to have come from the wreck of the Irish sailing ship the Faithful Steward, *are prized by collectors because of their romantic connotation.*[547]

Professional numismatists as well as "sophisticated collectors and writers"[548] were intrigued by the halfpennies showing up on Coin Beach. Few subjects are as esoteric as the study of copper money: scholarly tomes are filled with painstaking analyses of the hundreds of varieties of British and Irish halfpennies, real and fake, in circulation in the eighteenth and nineteenth centuries.[549] One numismatist declared that the sunken hulk of the *Faithful Steward* was a sort of "missing link" to the story of how a glut of rap pence made its way to the United States in 1785 and proof positive that the American economy was specifically targeted by coiners of counterfeit English and Irish halfpennies.[550]

Today, people still walk Coin Beach after strong Northeast storms in the hope that they will come across a *Faithful Steward* halfpenny. As though making amends for days of cold wind and rain off the ocean, the skies will clear, and the wind will come roaring in from the west. Light grains of sand are picked up off the beach and hurried back toward the Atlantic in smooth, tan sheets that reach the surf's edge, while bent blades of sea grass scribe perfect half circles on the dunes. Leaning against the wind, their heads down, beachcombers will sometimes come across a whimsical find uncovered by the wind: an old halfpenny standing on a damp little column of sand all its own, a dim image of King George III seeing the light of day for the first time in centuries.[551] On rare occasions, a beachcomber will find a shining gold guinea.

While these coins come from the same ship, they have different meanings. To find a halfpenny is to find a venerable old piece of commercial cargo. To find a guinea is to find a piece of an immigrant's dreams for the future.

NOTES

1. The Amateur Emigrant

1. McNally, "Weather of 1785," 58.
2. Dominguez-Castro, "Twelve Years of Daily Weather," 1531–47.
3. "Shipwreck of the Faithful Steward, At the Late McEntire and Mason Reunion on the Old McEntires Farm in East Fallowfield," *Crawford Journal–Meadville*, February 4, 1881
4. *History of Crawford County*, 543; Wenzel, *Ship Faithful Steward*, 80.
5. *Illustrated London News*, 230.
6. "Shipwreck of the Faithful Steward."
7. Stevenson, *Amateur Emigrant*, 21.
8. "Shipwreck of the Faithful Steward."
9. "The Faithful Steward: General Robert E. Lee's Ancestors, With a Strange Tale of Shipwreck," *(Philadelphia) Times*, December 6, 1885.
10. Goldenberg, *Shipbuilding in Colonial America*, 51, 69.
11. Coxe, *View of the United States*, 30–31.
12. Anonymous, *Remarks on Lord Sheffield's Observations*, 34, 40.
13. *Londonderry Journal*, May 10, 1785.
14. "Shipwreck of the Faithful Steward."
15. Thévenot, *Art of Swimming*, preface, 9.
16. *Londonderry Journal*, April 27, 1784.
17. *Londonderry Journal*, May 10, 1785.
18. *Londonderry Journal*, April 26, 1785.
19. *Londonderry Journal*, April 27, 1784.

20. *Londonderry Journal*, May 10, 1785.
21. *Londonderry Journal*, April 27, 1784.
22. *Belfast Newsletter*, August 16, 1785.
23. "Shipwreck of the Faithful Steward."
24. "The Predilection of America for Irish Commerce," *London-Derry Journal and General Advertiser*, August 3, 1784.
25. Wenzel, *Ship Faithful Steward*, 48.
26. O'Brien and Nolan, *Derry and Londonderry*, 513; Burke, *History of the Landed Gentry*, 1015.
27. *Londonderry Journal*, May 10, 1785
28. "Shipwreck of the Faithful Steward."

2. God Sends Meat and the Devil Cooks

29. Chandler, *Early Shipbuilding*, 32; Franklin, "Letter…to Rodolphe-Ferdinand Grand."
30. Sparks, *Familiar Letters*, 201.
31. Franklin, "Letter…to Rodolphe-Ferdinand Grand"; Jenkins, "Franklin Returns," 420–21.
32. Smyth, *Writings of Benjamin Franklin*, 372–405.
33. Franklin, "Letter…to Mr. Alphonsus le Roy," 322–23.
34. Van Doren, *Benjamin Franklin*, 188.
35. *Londonderry Journal*, April 27, 1784.
36. "Shipwreck of the Faithful Steward."
37. Franklin, "Letter…to Mr. Alphonsus le Roy," 328.
38. Anderson, *Radical Enlightenments*, 140.
39. *New Lloyd's List*, August 30, 1785.
40. "Shipwreck of the Faithful Steward."
41. Guillet, *Great Migration*, 66.
42. Ibid., 11.
43. Dickson, *Ulster Emigration*, 215.
44. Guillet, *Great Migration*, 11.
45. Anderson, *Sailing Ships*, 123–24.
46. Guillet, *Great Migration*, 72, 96.
47. Mooney, *Nine Years*, 48–49.
48. Guillet, *Great Migration*, 76.
49. MacKay, *Flight from Famine*, 209.
50. Stevens, *On the Stowage of Ships*, 784.

51. Ibid.
52. Guillet, *Great Migration*, 75.
53. Brown, *Poxed and Scurvied*, 129–30.
54. Wokeck, *Trade in Strangers*, 204.
55. Franklin, "Letter…to Mr. Alphonsus le Roy," 321–22.
56. Guillet, *Great Migration*, 114.
57. Stevenson, *Amateur Emigrant*, 4–5.
58. Franklin, "Letter…to Mr. Alphonsus le Roy," 322.
59. Mooney, *Nine Years*, 45–46.
60. Rose, *Canada in 1849*, 240.
61. Guillet, *Great Migration*, 57.
62. Mooney, *Nine Years*, 46.

3. A Fine Level Shore

63. *Port of Philadelphia*, 183.
64. *Pennsylvania Gazette*, November 12, 1761.
65. DeWire, *Lighthouses of the Mid-Atlantic Coast*, 24.
66. *Eighty-Eight Nautical Miles*, 8.
67. Coxe, *View of the United States of America*, 31.
68. Nelson, *Documents Relating to the Colonial History*, 445–46.
69. Putnam, *Lighthouses and Lightships*, 15.
70. Scharf, *History of Delaware*, 1225.
71. U.S. Department of the Treasury [hereafter Treasury], *Annual Report* (1867), 191.
72. Gillingham, "Lotteries in Philadelphia," 94.
73. *Pennsylvania Gazette*, September 10, 1767.
74. Scharf, *History of Delaware*, 1225.
75. Findlay, *Memoir Descriptive and Explanatory*, 775.
76. Treasury, *Report of the Officers Constituting the Light House Board*, 191–92.
77. *Pennsylvania Gazette*, September 8, 1773.
78. Manthorpe, "Lewes Lighthouse Legend Re-Examined."
79. "Sea Conquers Henlopen Light At Last," *New York Times*, March 21, 1926, 15.
80. *Pennsylvania Gazette*, February 11, 1784.
81. Findlay, *Memoir Descriptive and Explanatory*, 91–92.
82. Ibid., 93.
83. Purdy, *Columbian Navigator*, 105.

84. Treasury, *Annual Report* (1867), 33.

85. National Archives, "To Thomas Jefferson."

86. Treasury, *Annual Report* (1867), 35.

87. "At the Breakwater," *The Times*, July 20, 1878.

88. *Pennsylvania Gazette*, September 10, 1767.

89. Ackerman, *Notes from the Shore*, 4.

90. Wroten, *Assateague*, 52.

91. Groff, "Lost Settlement," 286.

92. Ackerman, *Notes from the Shore*, 4; Flook, *Native Americans*, 85.

93. Reiger, *Wanderer*, 98–101.

94. Bishop, *Voyage*, 122.

95. Furlong, *American Coast Pilot*, 55.

96. Lucas, *Chart of the Chesapeake and Delaware Bays*.

97. Dean, *Against the Tide*, 25.

98. Ibid.

99. Dalrymple, *Coastal Hydrodynamics*, 194.

100. Ibid., 184–85, 194, 317–19, 765–67.

101. Blunt, *American Coast Pilot* (18th ed.), 323.

102. Blunt, *American Coast Pilot* (12th ed.), 221.

103. U.S. Department of Commerce, National Oceanic and Atmospheric Administration, *United States Coast Pilot 3*, 95.

104. Furlong, *American Coast Pilot*, 55; Blunt, *American Coast Pilot* (18th ed.), 323; Hurley, *Shipwrecks and Rescues*, 114.

105. In Case. John Penn, "The Plaintiffs' Case," 2.

106. Purdy, *Columbian Navigator*, 105.

107. "A Dangerous Shore," *Buffalo Commercial*, November 16, 1892, 5.

108. *Pennsylvania Gazette*, September 10, 1767.

109. Treasury, *Report of the Secretary of the Treasury*, December 23, 1844, 22.

110. Risk, "Lamps, Maps, Mud-Machines," 40.

111. Scharf, *History of Delaware*, 1226.

112. Nanticoke Lenni-Lenape, "Our Tribal History."

113. Bishop, *Voyage*, 107–8.

114. Ibid., 108.

4. A Strange Humor

115. Dickson, *Ulster Emigration*, 205.

116. *Pennsylvania Packet and Daily Advertiser*, September 13, 1785.

117. Elliott, *Elliott Families*, 19.

118. Ibid.; "Faithful Steward."

119. Meginness, "Hepburn Family," 107.

120. Ibid., 107–8.

121. Lee, Duncan Campbell to Wm. Maxwell Scott Moore (letter), Public Record Office of Northern Ireland.

122. "Faithful Steward"; Elliott, *Elliott Families*, 19–20, 22; Schomette, *Shipwrecks*, 96.

123. "Faithful Steward."

124. *Pennsylvania Packet*, September 13, 1785; *Belfast Mercury*, November 22, 1785.

125. *Pennsylvania Packet*, September 13, 1785.

126. Elliott, *Elliott Families*, 20.

127. Mesick, *English Traveller*, 26–28.

128. Moody and Vaughan, *New History of Ireland*, 657–58.

129. King, *Thoughts on the Difficulties*, 6–7, 21.

130. Baseler, *Asylum for Mankind*, 168–69.

131. "Shipwreck of the Faithful Steward."

132. Dickson, *Ulster Emigration*, 64–66.

133. Wokeck, *Trade in Strangers*, 200–1.

134. Geiser, *Redemptioners and Indentured Servants*, 6–7.

135. Bric, "Ireland and Colonial America," 145.

136. Guillet, *Great Migration*, 34–35.

137. *Pennsylvania Gazette*, September 1, 1784.

138. Geiser, *Redemptioners and Indentured Servants*, 6–7.

139. Wokeck, *Trade in Strangers*, 187–88.

140. Baseler, *Asylum for Mankind*, 168.

141. Ibid., 171–77.

142. Griffin, "People with No Name," 1–4.

143. Baseler, *Asylum for Mankind*, 156–58.

144. Bailyn, *Voyagers to the West*, 40.

145. Baseler, *Asylum for Mankind*, 168–69.

146. Morton, *History of Rockbridge County*, 16.

147. "Shipwreck of the Faithful Steward."

148. Sigerson, *Modern Ireland*, 91–93.

149. Wells, *Ulster Migration*, 3–7.

150. Morton, *History of Rockbridge County*, 13–14.

151. Bardon, *Plantation of Ulster*, 3.

152. Wokeck, *Trade in Strangers*, 190.

153. Froude, *English in Ireland*, 275.

154. Joyce, *Concise History of Ireland*, 382–93; Froude, *English in Ireland*, 275; University of Minnesota, "Laws in Ireland."
155. Pinkerton, "Saint Patrick's Purgatory," 78.
156. Burke, *Works of Edmund Burke*, 343.
157. Morton, *History of Rockbridge County*, 15.
158. Bric, "Patterns of Irish Emigration," 8–9.
159. Morton, *History of Rockbridge County*, 15.
160. Kernohan, *County of Londonderry*, 50.
161. Bric, "Tithe System," 272.
162. Ibid., 277.
163. Ibid., 271.
164. Ibid., 282.
165. Bailyn, *Voyagers to the West*, 65.
166. Ibid., 43–48.
167. Mooney, *Nine Years in America*, 5.
168. Kernohan, *County of Londonderry*, 50.
169. Bric, "Patterns of Irish Emigration," 8–9.
170. "An Irishman's Diary on James McGregor, 'the Moses of the Scots Irish in America,'" *Irish Times*, January 3, 2018.
171. Kernohan, *County of Londonderry*, 49.
172. Wokeck, *Trade in Strangers*, 191.
173. Sanderson, *British Empire*, 99.
174. Joyce, *Concise History*, 395–97.
175. Tone, *An Argument*, 7.
176. Joyce, *Concise History of Ireland*, 397.
177. Great Britain, "House of Lords Journal Volume 17," 485–86.
178. King, *Thought on the Difficulties*, 38.
179. Bailyn, *Voyagers to the West*, 43–48.
180. National Archives, "From Benjamin Franklin to Thomas Cushing."
181. Bailyn, *Voyagers to the West*, 44.
182. Flynn and McCormack, *Westmeath 1798*, 6.
183. Boswell, *Life of Samuel Johnson*, 418.

5. Happy Mediocrity

184. Ibid.
185. Baseler, *Asylum for Mankind*, 157.
186. Fay, *Adam Smith*, 13.

187. Sheffield, *Observation on the Commerce*, 361–62.

188. Burke, *Select Works*, 178.

189. Ibid., 183.

190. Adams, *History of the United States*, 159–60.

191. Franklin, "Two Tracts."

192. Ibid., 3–4.

193. Rush, *Information to Europeans*, 3–4.

194. King, *Thought on the Difficulties*, 31–32.

195. Ibid., 31, 33.

196. Franklin, "Two Tracts," 5.

197. Ibid., 10–11.

198. Jefferson, *Notes on the State*, 172.

199. Anonymous, *Remarks on Lord Sheffield's Observations*, 42.

200. Rush, *Information to Europeans*, 7.

201. Franklin, "Two Tracts," 10.

202. Rush, *Information to Europeans*, 5.

203. Mooney, *Nine Years in America*, 37.

204. Henry, "On the Return," 7245.

205. Jefferson, *Notes on the State*, 89.

206. Ibid., 90.

207. Ibid., 172.

208. "From Prison to Post Office," *Bowery Boys*.

209. Dunn, *Discourse Delivered*, 11, 20, 28–29.

6. The Meteor

210. Jefferson, *Notes on the State*, 86.

211. *Pennsylvania Packet*, October 1, 1785; *Virginia Journal and Alexandria Advertiser*, October 13, 1785.

212. Johnson, "Meteor," *Dictionary of the English Language*.

213. Nelson, "Letter to Mrs. Nisbet, August 19, 1786," *Letters and Dispatches* [hereafter L&D], 188.

214. Toth, "Anglo-American Diplomacy," 424.

215. Nelson, "Letter to William Locker, September 4th, 1785," L&D, 138.

216. Ibid.; "Letter to William Locker, September 24th, 1785," L&D, 110.

217. *Pennsylvania Gazette*, October 5, 1785.

218. *Virginia Journal and Alexandria Advertiser*, October 13, 1785.

219. *Pennsylvania Packet*, October 12, 1785.

220. Ibid.
221. *Charleston Evening Gazette*, Saturday, October 8, 1785.
222. Tannehill, *Hurricanes*, 68.
223. *Pennsylvania Gazette*, October 5, 1785.
224. Nelson, "Letter to William Locker, September 4th, 1785," L&D, 138.
225. *Charleston Evening Gazette*, October 8 and October 14, 1785.
226. *Virginia Journal and Alexandria Advertiser*, Thursday, October 13, 1785.
227. *Pennsylvania Packet*, October 18, 1785.
228. *Pennsylvania Mercury*, October 14, 1785.
229. *Pennsylvania Packet*, October 4, 1785.
230. *Pennsylvania Gazette*, September 28, 1785.
231. *Charleston Evening Gazette*, October 14, 1785.
232. *Pennsylvania Packet*, October 29, 1785.
233. *Charleston Evening Gazette*, October 15, 1785; *Pennsylvania Evening Herald*, October 15, 1785.
234. *Pennsylvania Packet and Daily Advertiser*, October 13, 1785.
235. *Charleston Evening Gazette*, October 15, 1785
236. *Pennsylvania Evening Herald*, October 15, 1785.
237. *Pennsylvania Mercury*, Friday, October 14, 1785.
238. *Pennsylvania Packet*, October 13, 1785.
239. Purdy, *Memoir, Descriptive and Explanatory*, 142.
240. *Pennsylvania Packet and Daily Advertiser*, October 13, 1785.
241. *New Lloyd's List*, October 28, 1785; *Pennsylvania Evening Herald*, October 15, 1785.
242. *Pennsylvania Mercury*, Friday, October 14, 1785; *Pennsylvania Evening Herald*, October 15, 1785.
243. *Virginia Journal and Alexandria Advertiser*, October 27, 1785.
244. *Genuine Narrative*, 12.
245. *Pennsylvania Evening Herald*, October 15, 1785; *Charleston Evening Gazette*, October 15, 1785.
246. *Charleston Evening Gazette*, October 15, 1785.
247. *Pennsylvania Evening Herald*, October 12, 1785.
248. *Pennsylvania Mercury*, October 14, 1785.
249. *Pennsylvania Evening Herald*, October 15, 1785.
250. *Pennsylvania Mercury*, October 14, 1785.
251. *Pennsylvania Evening Herald*, October 15, 1785.
252. NOAA, "Saffir-Simpson Hurricane Wind Scale."
253. Purdy, *Memoir, Descriptive and Explanatory*, 135–36.
254. *Ladies Magazine*, 616.

255. *New Lloyd's List*, November 4, 1785.
256. Schwartz, *Hurricanes and the Middle Atlantic*, 46.
257. *Charleston Evening Gazette*, September 12 and 15, 1785.
258. Davis, et al., "North Atlantic Subtropical Cyclone," 728.
259. *Pennsylvania Mercury*, October 14, 1785.
260. Atherton, *Few of Hamilton's Letters*, 261–64.

7. Lost

261. Bedford, *Sailor's Handbook*, 35.
262. Jackson and Twohig, *Diaries of George Washington*, 188-89.
263. "Shipwreck of the Faithful Steward."
264. *Pennsylvania Gazette*, September 1, 1784.
265. Wokeck, *Trade in Strangers*, 198.

8. Rap Pence

266. Fitzpatrick, *Writings of George Washington*, 245–46.
267. Ibid., 248.
268. Jackson and Twohig, *Diaries of George Washington*, 183.
269. Ibid., 184.
270. Ibid.
271. Ibid., 188.
272. Ibid.
273. Ibid., 233.
274. Ibid.
275. Jefferson, *Notes on the State*, 178–79.
276. Kelby, "Notes on Coins," 116.
277. Ibid.
278. Ibid.
279. "O'Brien Coin Guide: Irish Evasion Halfpennies (1770s to the 1790s)," Old Currency Exchange, July 8, 2015, https://oldcurrencyexchange.com.
280. *Pennsylvania Gazette*, April 27, 1785.
281. *Pennsylvania Gazette*, October 27, 1773.
282. *Pennsylvania Gazette*, December 1789.
283. *Pennsylvania Gazette*, December 13, 1770; Kleeburg, "Shipwreck of the Faithful Steward," 90–91.

284. *Pennsylvania Gazette,* June 29, 1796.
285. *Pennsylvania Gazette,* May 18, 1769.
286. *Pennsylvania Gazette,* May 26, 1773.
287. *Pennsylvania Gazette,* February 10, 1773.
288. *Pennsylvania Gazette,* October 27, 1773.
289. *Pennsylvania Gazette,* February 10, 1773.
290. *Pennsylvania Gazette,* June 4, 1777.
291. *Pennsylvania Gazette,* August 9, 1780.
292. *Pennsylvania Gazette,* April 27, 1785.
293. *Pennsylvania Gazette,* November 22, 1750.
294. *Pennsylvania Gazette,* July 21, 1785.
295. *Pennsylvania Gazette,* May 16, 1771.
296. *Pennsylvania Gazette,* November 19, 1767.
297. *Pennsylvania Gazette,* November 1, 1770.
298. Newman, "Were Counterfeit British Style Halfpence," 207.
299. *Pennsylvania Evening Herald,* December 14, 1785.
300. Malone, *Critical and Miscellaneous Prose,* 294.
301. *Pennsylvania Gazette,* December 28, 1785.
302. Jordan, "Counterfeit British Coppers."
303. Ibid.
304. Ibid.
305. Ibid.
306. Scott, *Prose Works,* 20.
307. *Pennsylvania Gazette,* December 28, 1785.
308. *Charleston Evening Gazette,* September 14, 1785.
309. Newman, "Were Counterfeit British," 207, 217.
310. Kelby, "Notes on Coins," 117.
311. "Faithful Steward Wreck Is Topic Aug. 29 at Rehoboth Museum," *Cape Gazette,* August 23, 2019.
312. Jackson and Twohig, *Diaries of George Washington,* 189.
313. Ibid.

9. Petty Amphibious Tyrants

314. "Shipwreck of the Faithful Steward."
315. Dickson, *Ulster Emigration,* 249.
316. "Shipwreck of the Faithful Steward."
317. Franklin, "Letter…to Mr. Alphonsus le Roy," 320.

318. Gompers, "Free and Skilled Seamen," 1037.

319. Book of Common Prayer, "At the Burial of Their Dead at Sea."

320. MacKay, *Flight from Famine*, 209.

321. Vandeburgh, *Mariner's Medical Guide*, 54.

322. Dickson, *Ulster Emigration*, 209.

323. Guillet, *Great Migration*, 18.

324. Mooney, *Nine Years in America*, 51.

325. *Pennsylvania Evening Herald*, October 26, 1785.

326. *Londonderry Journal*, February 28, 1786.

327. Perkins, *Treatise of the Law*, 310.

328. Gompers, "Free and Skilled Seamen," 1037.

329. Jack, "Why Must a Captain."

330. Knight, *Modern Seamanship*, 632–33.

331. *Tales of Heroism*, 454.

332. Grosh, *Evangelical Magazine*, 136.

333. Harris, "Shipwreck Off Hatteras," 76.

334. Elinder and Erixson, "Gender, Social Norms," 13221.

335. Ibid.

336. Mooney, *Nine Years*, 50–52.

337. Elinder and Erixson, "Gender, Social Norms," 13220.

338. Ibid., 13223.

339. Ibid., 13222.

340. *Pennsylvania Packet*, September 13, 1785.

341. "Shipwreck of the Faithful Steward."

342. *Pennsylvania Gazette*, September 13, 1785.

10. The Voracious Deep

343. Sharp, "Artificial Beach Construction," 35; Dean, *Against the Tide*, 155–56.

344. Shepard, *Lore of the Wreckers*, 5, 7.

345. "Shipwreck of the Faithful Steward."

346. Ibid.

347. Guillet, *Great Migration*, 81, 83.

348. "Lightship Beacons," *New York Times*, February 3, 1913; Harris, "Shipwreck Off Hatteras," 75–79.

349. Treasury, *Annual Report* (1877), 16.

350. "Shipwreck of the Faithful Steward."

351. Franklin, "Letter…to Mr. Alphonsus le Roy," 328.

352. Guillet, *Great Migration*, 39-40.

353. Brody, "Surviving the Cold."

354. Vanderbilt, "Crisis."

355. Madsen et al., "Effects of Detraining," 1444; Martin et al., "Effects of Physical Deconditioning," 982, 987.

356. Australian Psychological Society, "Psychological Preparation," 2.

357. "Shipwreck of the Faithful Steward."

358. Ibid.

359. Harris, "Shipwreck Off Hatteras," 76.

360. Whymper, *Sea*, 51.

361. "Shipwreck of the Faithful Steward."

362. *Pennsylvania Packet*, September 13, 1785.

363. "Shipwreck of the Faithful Steward."

364. Ibid.

365. U.S. Department of State, "International Convention," 199.

366. Welshman, *Titanic*, 109.

367. "Shipwreck of the Faithful Steward."

368. *The Times*, November 24, 1785; *Daily Universal Register*, November 24, 1785. See also *Pennsylvania Gazette*, September 13, 1785; *Pennsylvania Packet*, September 13, 1785.

369. Lawson, *Record of the Shipping*, 223.

370. Johnson, "Boatswain," *Dictionary of the English Language*.

371. Swain, interview with the author, August 10, 2000.

372. *Pennsylvania Packet*, September 13, 1785.

373. "Shipwreck of the Faithful Steward."

374. Ibid.

375. *Pennsylvania Packet*, September 12 and 13, 1785.

376. "Shipwreck of the Faithful Steward."

377. Ibid.

378. Ibid.

379. Treasury, *Annual Report* (1892), 21.

380. Ibid., 23.

381. Tanber, "Forgotten Maritime Tragedy."

382. Treasury, *Annual Report* (1892), 23.

383. Bailey, "To Stave," *Universal Etymological English Dictionary*.

384. "Ground-Swell Goblin!" 26.

385. Lawson, *Record of the Shipping*, 140.

386. Swain, interview with the author, August 10, 2000.

387. Dolan and Davis, "Intensity Scale," 843–45.
388. Surf Channel, "How Heavy Are the Biggest Waves."
389. Cox et al., "Extraordinary Boulder Transport," 625.
390. Ibid., 623–36; Cox, Zentner, et al., "Boulder Ridges," 249–72.
391. Cleghorn, *Hydo-Aëronaut*, 52.
392. Purdy, *Memoir, Descriptive and Explanatory*, 137.
393. Ibid., 149.
394. London, *Two Months on the Tobique*, 30.
395. Harris, "Shipwreck Off Hatteras," 77.
396. Markham, "Letter from the Chief," 18.
397. Dean, "Stalking a Killer."
398. "Shipwreck of the Faithful Steward."
399. Ibid.
400. Treasury, *Annual Report* (1877), 21.
401. "Shipwreck of the Faithful Steward."
402. Wokeck, *Trade in Strangers*, 205.
403. "Faithful Steward," *The Times*.
404. "Shipwreck of the Faithful Steward."
405. Meginness, "Hepburn Family," 108.
406. "Shipwreck of the Faithful Steward."
407. Ibid.
408. Ibid.
409. Chesler, "Do Serious Beach Injuries."
410. California State Parks, "Refugio Junior Lifeguards Assistant Training Manual."
411. "Shipwreck of the Faithful Steward."
412. Ibid.

11. Outlaws and Vagabonds

413. Ibid.
414. Ibid.
415. Thoreau, *Cape Cod*, 7–8.
416. Robinson and Robinson, *New Annual Register*, 87.
417. Porter, "Lay Medical Knowledge," 151; Brown, "Healthcare During Lucy's Lifetime."
418. Buchan, *Domestic Medicine*, 342, 426; Royle, *Materia Medica*, 559, 666.
419. "Shipwreck of the Faithful Steward."

420. Ibid.

421. Thomas, *Swimming*, 15.

422. "Shipwreck of the Faithful Steward."

423. *Pennsylvania Packet*, September 24, 1785.

424. Stick, *Graveyard of the Atlantic*, 4.

425. *Pennsylvania Gazette*, March 13, 1766; Nelson, *Documents*, 50–51.

426. Turner, *Some Records*, 221.

427. Ibid.

428. Ibid., 221, 237.

429. Ibid., 358.

430. Federal Writers' Project, *Delaware*, 500.

431. Stick, *Graveyard of the Atlantic*, 11.

432. Jenkin, *Cornish Seafarers*, 98.

433. Pollock, *Essay on Possession*, 1.

434. Bathurst, *Wreckers*, 269.

435. Jenkin, *Cornish Seafarers*, 117.

436. Stick, *Graveyard of the Atlantic*, 4.

437. Schneider, *Enduring Shore*, 205–7.

438. "Old Colonial Drinks and Drinkers," 154.

439. Jenkin, *Cornish Seafarers*, 85.

440. Ibid., 87.

441. Morison, *Maritime History*, 7.

442. Schneider, *Enduring Shore*, 205–7.

443. Jenkin, *Cornish Seafarers*, 76-77.

444. "Shipwreck of the Faithful Steward."

445. Ibid.

446. Ibid.

447. Ibid.

448. Lee, Duncan Campbell, to Wm. Maxwell Scott Moore, Public Record Office of Northern Ireland; "Faithful Steward," *The Times*; *Londonderry Journal*, February 28, 1786.

449. *Londonderry Journal*, February 28, 1786; Elliott, *Elliott Families*, 19.

450. *Pennsylvania Packet*, September 13, 1785.

451. "Shipwreck of the Faithful Steward."

452. Elliott, *Elliott Families*, 21.

453. "Shipwreck of the Faithful Steward."

454. Ibid.

455. Ibid.

456. Turner, *Some Records*, 196–97.

457. "Shipwreck of the Faithful Steward."

458. Ibid.

459. Ibid.

460. Ibid.

461. Ibid.

462. *Inventory of the County Archives of Pennsylvania*, 13.

463. *Philadelphia Journal and Weekly Advertiser*, September 14, 1785·

464. "Faithful Steward," *The Times*.

465. Ibid.

466. Ford, *Commerce of Rhode Island*, 268–70.

467. *Pennsylvania Packet*, September 15, 1785; *Charleston Evening Gazette*, October 8, 1785.

468. *Pennsylvania Packet*, September 16, 1785.

469. *Londonderry Journal*, November 22, 1785.

470. *Pennsylvania Evening Herald*, January 7, 1786; *Londonderry Journal*, February 28, 1786.

471. "Shipwreck of the Faithful Steward."

12. Red Clover

472. Armstrong Economics, "US Population."

473. "Shipwreck of the Faithful Steward."

474. Ibid.

475. Eaton, *History of the Presbytery*, 145.

476. "Shipwreck of the Faithful Steward."

477. Ibid.

478. American College of Occupational and Environmental Medicine, "Practice Resources," https://acoem.org.

479. "Shipwreck of the Faithful Steward."

480. Elliott, *Elliott Families*, 21.

481. "Faithful Steward," *The Times*.

482. "Shipwreck of the Faithful Steward."

483. *History of Crawford County*, 622.

484. "Shipwreck of the Faithful Steward."

485. Ibid.

486. *History of Crawford County*, 622; "Shipwreck of the Faithful Steward."

487. *Combination Atlas Map*, 26.

488. *History of Crawford County*, 622.

489. "Shipwreck of the Faithful Steward."
490. *History of Crawford County*, 622.
491. Ibid., 645.
492. "Shipwreck of the Faithful Steward."
493. Franklin, "Two Tracts," 5.
494. Webster, "Mediocrity," *American Dictionary*.
495. "Shipwreck of the Faithful Steward."
496. Ibid.
497. Ibid.; *Combination Atlas Map*, 26.

13. Money Beach

498. Spears, "Sand-Waves," 509.
499. Treasury, *Report of the Secretary* (1868), 347.
500. Treasury, "Letter from the Secretary."
501. "Sea Conquers," *New York Times*.
502. Treasury, *Report of the Secretary* (1868), 347.
503. Mints, *Angels in the Night*, 70.
504. Treasury, *Report of the Secretary* (1868), 149.
505. Treasury, *Report of the Secretary* (1868), 347.
506. Ibid.
507. "Timber Bulkheads," 771.
508. Department of Commerce, "Annual Report of the Commissioner of Lighthouses [1920]," 72.
509. Appropriations, Department of Commerce, *Hearing Before the Subcommittee*, 166.
510. U.S. Department of Agriculture, "Climatological Data," 15–16.
511. Roales, *Delaware Lighthouses*, 15.
512. Federal Writers' Project, *Delaware*, 413.
513. Ibid., 412.
514. Dean, *Against the Tide*, 90; Markum, "Letter from the Chief," 5.
515. Pillsbury, "Report of the Board," 4.
516. Federal Writers' Project, *Delaware*, 412.
517. Pillsbury, "Report of the Board," 3.
518. Horowitz, "History of the Indian River Inlet."
519. Markum, "Letter from the Chief," 7, 21–22.
520. Ibid., 33.
521. Ibid., 23.
522. Pittenger, "River and Harbor Bill," 184.

523. Markum, "Letter from the Chief," 23.
524. Morgan, "Indian River Inlet," *Delmarva Now*, May 25, 2019; Horowitz, "History of the Indian River Inlet."
525. Ibid.
526. Markum, "Letter from the Chief," 23.
527. Ibid., 1.
528. Ibid., 24.
529. Ibid., 5.
530. U.S. Army Corps of Engineers, "Indian River Inlet."
531. Page, *Delaware in the Great Depression*, 105–7.
532. "Find George III Coins," *New York Times*, February 23, 1937.
533. Federal Writers' Project, *Delaware*, 411–12; Schomette, *Shipwrecks*, 94.
534. International Association of Dredging Companies, "Facts About Cutter Suction Dredgers," https://www.iadc-dredging.com.
535. "Coins of 1749–1775," *New York Times*.
536. "Waves Deposit Coins of Early 18th Century," *Republican and Herald*, March 4, 1938.
537. Ibid.
538. Mooney, *Nine Years*, 47.
539. Guillet, *Great Migration*, 37.
540. "Dredging Work at Inlet," *Smyrna Times*, June 24, 1938; "Warwick," *Milford Chronicle*, June 24, 1938.
541. "Treasure Ship Swept to Sea," *Smyrna Times*, October 27, 1938.
542. "Lewes," *Milford Chronicle*, September 16, 1938.
543. "Treasure Ship Swept to Sea," *Smyrna Times*.
544. "Waves Deposit Coins," *Republican and Herald*.
545. *New York Times*, July 14, 1857, 2.
546. Trupp, *Tracking Treasure*, 201.
547. "Storm Reveals Old Coins," *New York Times*, September 1, 1939.
548. Newman, "Were Counterfeit British," 210, 217; Kleeburg, "Shipwreck of the Faithful Steward," 55–77.
549. Newman, "Were Counterfeit British," 210.
550. Kleeburg, "Shipwreck of the Faithful Steward," 56.
551. Brown, "Long Beach Island."

BIBLIOGRAPHY

Ackerman, Jennifer. *Notes from the Shore*. New York: Viking, 1995.

Adams, Henry. *History of the United States of America During the First Administration of Thomas Jefferson*. Vol. 1. New York: Charles Scribner's Sons, 1909.

Anderson, Douglas. *The Radical Enlightenments of Benjamin Franklin*. Baltimore: Johns Hopkins University Press, 1997.

Anderson, Ernest. *Sailing Ships of Ireland*. Dublin: Morris and Company, 1951.

Anonymous. *Remarks on Lord Sheffield's Observations on the Commerce of the American States; By an American*. London: John Stockdale, 1784.

Appropriations, Department of Commerce. *Hearing Before the Subcommittee of House Committee on Appropriations*. 68th Cong., 2nd Sess. Washington, D.C.: Government Printing Office, 1925.

Armstrong Economics. "US Population 1776–Date." https://www.armstrongeconomics.com.

Atherton, Gertrude ed. *A Few of Hamilton's Letters*. London: MacMillan & Company, 1903.

Australian Psychological Society. "Psychological Preparation for Natural Disasters." https://psychology.org.au.

Bailey, Nathan. *An Universal Etymological English Dictionary*. 20th ed. London: 1773.

Bailyn, Bernard. *Voyagers to the West, A Passage in the Peopling of America on the Eve of the Revolution*. New York: Alfred A. Knopf, 1986.

Bardon, Jonathan. *The Plantation of Ulster: War and Conflict in Ireland*. Dublin: Gill Books, 2011.

Baseler, Marilyn. *Asylum for Mankind: America, 1607–1800*. Ithaca, NY: Cornell University Press, 1998.

Bathurst, Bella. *The Wreckers: A Story of Killing Seas and Plundered Shipwrecks, from the 18th Century to Today*. Boston: Houghton Mifflin Company, 2005.

Bedford, F.G.D. *The Sailor's Handbook*. Portsmouth: Griffin & Co., 1890.

Bishop, Nathaniel. *Voyage of the Paper Canoe*. Boston: Lee and Shepard, 1878.

Blunt, Edmund. *The American Coast Pilot: Containing Directions for the Principal Harbours, Capes, and Headlands on the Coast of North and South America*. 12th ed. New York: Edmund and George W. Blunt, 1833.

————. *The American Coast Pilot: Containing Directions for the Principal Harbours, Capes, and Headlands on the Coast of North and South America*. 18th ed. New York: Edmund and George W. Blunt, 1857.

The Book of Common Prayer. "At the Burial of Their Dead at Sea." London: Church of England, 1681.

Boswell, James. *The Life of Samuel Johnson*, vol. 1. New York: George Dearborn & Company, 1837.

Bowery Boys (blog). "From Prison to Post Office: The Odd Fate of a Dutch Church." February 9, 2012, www.boweryboyshistory.com.

Bric, Maurice. "Ireland and Colonial America: The Viewer and the Viewed." In *European Encounters: Essays in Memory of Albert Lovett*, edited by Judith Devlin and Howard B. Clarke, 145. Dublin: University College Dublin Press, 2003.

————. "Patterns of Irish Emigration to America, 1783–1800." In *New Directions in Irish-American History*, edited by Kevin Kenney, 8–9. Madison: University of Wisconsin Press, 2003.

————. "The Tithe System in Eighteenth-Century Ireland." Proceedings of the Royal Irish Academy. Section C: Archaeology, Celtic Studies, History, Linguistics, Literature 86C (1986): 271–88.

Brody, Jane. "Surviving the Cold, or Not So Cold." *New York Times*, January 9, 2007.

Brown, Edward. "Long Beach Island: Monetary Dividends." *New York Times*, August 29, 1976.

Brown, Eileen B. Malone. "Healthcare During Lucy's Lifetime." *Lucy Meriwether Lewis Marks, A Biographical and Botanical Art Exhibit*. Monticello, VA: Jefferson Library, 2009. https://www.monticello.org.

Brown, Kevin. *Poxed and Scurvied: The Story of Health and Sickness at Sea*. Barnsley, UK: Seaforth Publishing, 2011.

Buchan, William. *Domestic Medicine, or the Family Physician*. 2nd American ed. Philadelphia: Printed by Joseph Crukshank, 1774.

Burke, Bernard. *History of the Landed Gentry of Great Britain & Ireland*. Vol. 2. 6th ed. London: Harrison, 1882.

Burke, Edmund. *Burke, Select Works*. Vol. 1. Edited by E.J. Payne. Oxford: Clarendon Press, 1892–98.

———. *The Works of Edmund Burke*. Vol. 3. London: George Bell and Sons, 1903.

California State Parks, Channel Coast District/Santa Barbara Sector. "Refugio Junior Lifeguards Assistant Training Manual." https://www.parks.ca.gov.

Chandler, Charles Lyon. *Early Shipbuilding in Pennsylvania, 1683–1812*. Philadelphia: Colonial Press, 1932.

Chesler, Caren. "Do Serious Beach Injuries Come in Waves?" *Scientific American*, June 7, 2013.

Cleghorn, Thomas. *The Hydo-Aëronaut, or Navigator's Life-Buoy*. London: Mercier and Chervet, 1810.

Combination Atlas Map of Crawford County, Pennsylvania. Philadelphia: Everts, Ensign & Evert, 1876.

Coxe, Tench. *A View of the United States of America*. Philadelphia: William Hall, 1794.

Cox, Rónadh, Danielle B. Zentner, Brian J. Kirchner and Mea S. Cook. "Boulder Ridges on the Aran Islands (Ireland): Recent Movements Caused by Storm Waves, Not Tsunamis." *Journal of Geology* 120, no. 3 (May 2012): 249–72.

Cox, Rónadh, Kalle L. Jahn, Oona G. Watkins and Peter Cox. "Extraordinary Boulder Transport by Storm Waves (West of Ireland, Winter 2013–2014), and Criteria for Analysing Coastal Boulder Deposits." *Earth Science Reviews* 177 (February 2018): 623–36.

Dalrymple, Robert A., ed. *Coastal Hydrodynamics*. New York: American Society of Civil Engineers, 1987.

Davis, Robert E., Bruce P. Hayden, David A. Gay and William L. Phillips. "The North Atlantic Subtropical Cyclone." *Journal of Climate* 10 (April 1997): 728–44.

Dean, Cornelia. *Against the Tide, The Battle for America's Beaches*. New York: Columbia University Press, 1999.

———. "Stalking a Killer That Lurks a Few Feet Offshore." *New York Times*, June 7, 2005.

Department of Commerce, Bureau of Lighthouses. "Annual Report of the Commissioner of Lighthouses to the Secretary of Commerce for the Fiscal Year Ended June 30, 1920." Washington, D.C.: Government Printing Office, 1920.

DeWire, Elinor. *Lighthouses of the Mid-Atlantic Coast: Your Guide to the Lighthouses of New York, New Jersey, Maryland, Delaware, and Virginia.* Stillwater, MN: Voyageur Press, 2002.

Dickson, R.J. *Ulster Emigration to Colonial America 1718–1775.* Belfast: Ulster Historical Foundation, 1966.

Dolan, Robert, and Robert E. Davis. "An Intensity Scale for Atlantic Coast Northeast Storms." *Journal of Coastal Research* 8, no. 4 (Fall 1992): 840–53.

Dominguez-Castro, Fernando. "Twelve Years of Daily Weather Descriptions in North America in the Eighteenth Century (Mexico City, 1775–86)." *Bulletin of the American Meteorological Society* (August 2019): 1531–47.

Dunn, Thomas. *A Discourse Delivered in the New Dutch Church, Nassau Street, on Tuesday, the 21st of October, 1794, Before the New York Society for the Information and Assistance of Persons Emigrating from Foreign Countries.* New York: L. Wayland, 1794.

Eaton, Samuel John Mills. *History of the Presbytery of Erie.* New York: Hurd & Houghton, 1868.

Eighty-Eight Nautical Miles on the Delaware. Philadelphia: Philadelphia Maritime Exchange, 1950.

Elinder, Mikael, and Oscar Erixson. "Gender, Social Norms, and Survival in Maritime Disasters." *Proceedings of the National Academy of Sciences* 109, no. 33 (August 2012): 13220–24.

Elliott, Simon. *The Elliott Families.* Chicago: Press of Stevens, Maloney and Company, 1911.

Fay, C.R. *Adam Smith and the Scotland of His Day.* Cambridge: Cambridge University Press, 1956.

Federal Writers' Project of the Works Progress Administration. *Delaware: A Guide to the First State.* New York: Viking Press, 1938.

Findlay, Alexander George. *Memoir Descriptive and Explanatory, of the Northern Atlantic Ocean, and Comprising Instructions, General and Particular, for the Navigation of that Sea.* 14th ed. London: Richard Holmes Laurie, 1879.

Fitzpatrick, John, ed. *The Writings of George Washington, from the Original Manuscript Sources, 1745–1799*, vol. 28, *December 5, 1784–August 30, 1786.* Washington, D.C.: U.S. Government Printing Office, 1931–44.

Flook, Chris. *Native Americans of East-Central Indiana.* Charleston, SC: The History Press, 2016.

Flynn, Kathleen, and Stan McCormack. *Westmeath 1798: A Kilbeggan Rebellion.* Ireland: K. Flynn & S. McCormack, 1998.

Ford, Worthington Chauncey, ed. *Commerce of Rhode Island, 1726–1800.* Vol. 2. Boston: Plimpton Press, 1915.

Franklin, Benjamin. "Letter from Benjamin Franklin to Rodolphe-Ferdinand Grand, Rouen, July 16. 1785." The Papers of Benjamin Franklin, Sponsored by the American Philosophical Society and Yale University, Digital Edition, Packard Humanities Institute.

———. "A Letter from Dr. Benjamin Franklin to Mr. Alphonsus le Roy, Member of Several Academies at Paris, Containing Sundry Maritime Observations." In *Transactions of the American Philosophical Society*, vol. 2. Philadelphia, 1786.

———. "Two Tracts: Information to Those Who Would Remove to America and Remarks Concerning the Savages of North America." Dublin: Printed for L. White, 1784.

Froude, James Anthony. *The English in Ireland in the Eighteenth Century*. Vol. 1. New York: Charles Scribner's Sons, 1888.

Furlong, Lawrence. *The American Coast Pilot*. 1st ed. Newburyport, MA: Blunt and March, 1796.

Geiser, Karl Frederick. *Redemptioners and Indentured Servants in the Colony and Commonwealth of Pennsylvania*. New Haven, CT: Yale Publishing Company, 1901.

The Genuine Narrative of the Life and Transactions of Major Maurice Keating. London: Printed by J. Miller, 1785.

Gillingham, Harold. "Lotteries in Philadelphia Prior to 1776." *Pennsylvania History: A Journal of Mid-Atlantic Studies* 5, no. 2 (April 1938).

Goldenberg, Joseph. *Shipbuilding in Colonial America*. Newport News: University Press of Virginia for the Mariners Museum, 1976.

Gompers, Samuel. "Free and Skilled Seamen Insure Safety At Sea." *American Federationist* 20, part 2 (January 1913): 1037.

Great Britain. "House of Lords Journal Volume 17: 17 March 1704." In *Journal of the House of Lords*, vol. 17, *1701–1705*. London: His Majesty's Stationery Office, 1767–1830.

Griffin, Patrick. "The People with No Name: Ulster's Migrants and Identity Formation in Eighteenth Century Pennsylvania." *William and Mary Quarterly* 58, no. 3 (July 2001): 1–4.

Groff, George. "A Lost Settlement of the Delaware." In *Some Records of Sussex County Delaware*, edited by C.H.B. Turner. Philadelphia: Allen, Lane & Scott, 1909.

Grosh, Aaron ed. *Evangelical Magazine and Gospel Advocate*. Vol. 1. Utica, NY: A.B. & C.C.P. Grosh, Publishers, 1840.

"The Ground-Swell Goblin!" *Illustrated Sailors Magazine and New Nautical Miscellany*, February–July 1845.

Guillet, Edwin. *The Great Migration*: *The Atlantic Crossing by Sailing-Ship Since 1770*. New York: Thomas Nelson and Sons, 1937.

Harris, Sarah Kollock. "Shipwreck Off Hatteras." In *An Outer Banks Reader*, edited by David Stick, 75–79. Chapel Hill: University of North Carolina Press, 1998.

Henry, Patrick. "On the Return of the Refugees." In *A Library of the World's Best Literature Ancient and Modern*, edited by Charles Dudley Warner. New York: The International Society, 1897.

History of Crawford County, Pennsylvania. Chicago: Warner, Beers & Co. 1885.

Horowitz, Kenneth. "History of the Indian River Inlet at Delaware Seashore State Park." *Delaware State Parks Adventure* (blog), February 24, 2020. https://destateparks.blog.

Hurley, George, and Suzanne Hurley. *Shipwrecks and Rescues Along the Barrier Islands of Delaware, Maryland, and Virginia*. Norfolk, VA: Donning Company/Publishers, 1984.

The Illustrated London News, vol. 3, *July 1–December 30, 1843*. London: William Little, 1844.

Inventory of the County Archives of Pennsylvania. Prepared by the Pennsylvania Historical Records Survey Division of Professional and Service Projects, Works Projects Administration. Lancaster County, No. 36. Lancaster County, PA: Board of County Commissioners, February 1941.

Jack, Ian. "Why Must a Captain Never Leave a Sinking Ship?" *The Guardian*, January 20, 2012.

Jackson, Donald, and Dorothy Twohig, eds. *The Diaries of George Washington*. Charlottesville: University Press of Virginia, 1976.

Jefferson, Thomas. *Notes on the State of Virginia*. Boston: Lilly and Wait, 1832.

Jenkin, Alfred Kenneth Hamilton. *Cornish Seafarers, The Smuggling, Wrecking and Fishing Life of Cornwall*. London: J.M. Dent & Sons Ltd., 1932.

Jenkins, Charles. "Franklin Returns from France—1785." *Proceedings of the American Philosophical Society* 92, no. 6 (December 1948): 417–32.

Johnson, Samuel. *A Dictionary of the English Language*. 3rd ed. Dublin: W.G. Jones, 1768.

Jordan, Louis. "Counterfeit British Coppers: Introduction." Coin and Currency Collections at the University of Notre Dame Department of Special Collections. https://coins.nd.edu.

Joyce, Patrick Weston. *A Concise History of Ireland*. London: Longmans, Green and Company, 1903.

Kelby, William. "Notes on Coins." In *The Historical Magazine, and Notes and Queries Concerning the Antiquities, History, and Biography of America*. Vol. 5. 2nd series. Morrisania, NY: Henry B. Dawson, 1869.

Kernohan, J.W. *The County of Londonderry in Three Centuries*. Belfast: Published by the author, 1921.

King, John. *Thoughts on the Difficulties and Distresses in Which the Peace of 1783 Has Involved the People of England*. 5th ed. London: T. Davies, 1783.

Kleeburg, John M. "The Shipwreck of the Faithful Steward: A 'Missing Link' in the Export of British and Irish Halfpence." In *Coinage of the American Confederation Period: Coinage of the Americas Conference at the American Numismatic Society, October 28, 1995*, edited by Philip L. Mossman, 55–77. New York: American Numismatic Society, 1996.

Knight, Austin Melvin. *Modern Seamanship*. 7th ed. New York: D. Van Nostrand Company, 1918.

The Ladies Magazine or Entertaining Companion for the Fair Sex. Vol. 16. London: G. Robinson, 1785.

Lawson, J. Murray. *Record of the Shipping of Yarmouth, N.S.* St. Johns, New Brunswick: J. & A. McMillan, 1876.

Lee, Duncan Campbell, to Wm. Maxwell Scott Moore, Esq., September 13, 1933. Public Record Office of Northern Ireland MIC/60/5.

London, M.C.S. *Two Months on the Tobique, New Brunswick: An Emigrant's Journal*. London: Smith, Elder and Co., 1866.

Lucas, Fielding. *A Chart of the Chesapeake and Delaware Bays*. Philadelphia: 1862.

MacKay, Donald. *Flight from Famine: The Coming of the Irish to Canada*. Toronto: Natural Heritage Books, 2009.

Madsen, Kenneth, P.K. Pedersen, M.S. Djurhuus and N.A. Klitgaard. "Effects of Detraining on Endurance Capacity and Metabolic Changes During Prolonged Exhaustive Exercise." *Journal of Applied Physiology* 75, no. 4 (October 1993): 1444–51.

Malone, Edmond, ed. *The Critical and Miscellaneous Prose Works of John Dryden*. Vol. 2. London: Cadell and Davies, 1800.

Manthorpe, William. "The Lewes Lighthouse Legend Re-Examined and Re-Interpreted." *Journal of the American Revolution* (November 2019). https://allthingsliberty.com.

Markham, E.M. "Letter from the Chief of Engineers, United States Army, Transmitting Report of the Boards of Engineers for Rivers and Harbors on Review of Reports Heretofore Submitted on Indian River Inlet and Bay, Del., with Illustration," July 7, 1937. 75th Congress, 1st Sess., Committee on Rivers and Harbors, House of Representatives, Doc. No. 41.

Martin, Wade, E.F. Coyle, S.A. Bloomfields and A.A. Ehsani. "Effects of Physical Deconditioning After Intense Endurance Training on Left Ventricular Dimensions and Stroke Volume." *Journal of the American College of Cardiology* 7, no. 5 (May 1986): 982–89.

McNally, Louis. "The Weather of 1785: An Interdisciplinary Approach to Meteorological Reconstruction Using Forensic Synoptic Analysis." PhD. Diss., University of Maine, 2004.

Meginness, John. "The Hepburn Family." *Historical Journal: A Quarterly Record of Local History and Genealogy* 2, no. 2 (1894).

Mesick, Jane Louise. *The English Traveller in America, 1785–1835.* New York: Columbia University Press, 1922.

Mints, Margaret Louise. *Angels in the Night, Lighthouses of New Jersey and Delaware.* Port Norris, NJ: Mints and Ogden, 1995.

Moody, T.W., and W.E. Vaughan, eds. *A New History of Ireland.* Vol. 4. Oxford: Clarendon Press, 1986.

Mooney, Thomas. *Nine Years in America.* Dublin: James McGlashan, 1850.

Morgan, Michael. "Indian River Inlet: A Cantankerous Waterway." *Delmarva Now,* May 25, 2019.

Morison, Samuel Eliot. *The Maritime History of Massachusetts, 1783–1860.* Boston: Houghton Mifflin Company, 1921.

Morton, Oren Frederic. *A History of Rockbridge County, Virginia.* Staunton, VA: McClure Co., 1920.

The Nanticoke Lenni-Lenape. "Our Tribal History." https://nanticoke-lenape.info/history.htm.

National Archives. "From Benjamin Franklin to Thomas Cushing, 13 January 1772." *Founders Online,* https://founders.archives.gov.

———. "Information to Those Who Would Remove to America [Before March 1784]." *Founders Online,* https://founders.archives.gov.

———. "To Thomas Jefferson from Abraham Hargis, 26 May 1802." *Founders Online,* https://founders.archives.gov.

National Oceanic and Atmospheric Administration, National Hurricane Center. "Saffir-Simpson Hurricane Wind Scale." https://www.nhc.noaa.gov/aboutsshws.php.

Nelson, Horatio. *The Letters and Dispatches of Vice Admiral Lord Viscount Nelson,* vol. 1, *1777–1794.* London: Henry Colburn, 1845.

Nelson, William, ed. *Documents Relating to the Colonial History of the State of New Jersey,* vol. 25, *1766–1767.* Paterson, NJ: Call Printing and Publishing, 1908.

Newman, Eric. "Were Counterfeit British Style Halfpence Dated 1785 Made Specifically for American Use?" Museum Notes, *American Numismatic Society* 33 (1988).

O'Brien, Gerard, and William Noland, eds. *Derry and Londonderry: History & Society*. Dublin: Geography Publications, 1999.

"Old Colonial Drinks and Drinkers." *National Magazine, A Journal Devoted to American History* 16, no. 1 (May 1892).

Page, R. Brian. *Delaware in the Great Depression*. Charleston, SC: Arcadia Publishing, 2005.

Perkins, J.C. *Treatise of the Law Relative to Merchant Ships and Seamen in Five Parts*. Boston: Little, Brown and Company, 1854.

Penn vs. Baltimore. *In Case. John Penn, Thomas Penn, and Richard Penn, Esqrs. Plaintiffs. Charles Calvert Esq; Lord Baltimore in the Kingdom of Ireland. Defendant. The Plaintiffs Case*. [1743]. https://www.loc.gov/item/2005577765/.

Pillsbury, G.B. "Report of the Board of Engineers for Rivers and Harbors," June 23, 1937. 75th Congress, 1st Sess., Committee on Rivers and Harbors, House of Representatives, Doc. No. 41.

Pinkerton, William. "Saint Patrick's Purgatory. Part IV. Modern History." *Ulster Journal of Archaeology* 5 (1857).

Pittenger, Rep. William Alvin. "River and Harbor Bill." September 18, 1941. 77th Cong., 2nd Sess. Washington, D.C.: U.S. Government Printing Office, 1942.

Pollock, Frederick. *An Essay on Possession in Common Law*. Oxford: Clarendon Press, 1888.

Porter, R. "Lay Medical Knowledge in the Eighteenth Century: The Evidence of the Gentleman's Magazine." *Medical History* 29, no. 2 (April 1985): 138–68.

The Port of Philadelphia, Its History, Advantages, and Facilities. Philadelphia: Department of Wharves, Docks and Ferries, 1926.

Purdy, John. *The Columbian Navigator; or, Sailing Directory for the American Coasts and West Indies*. London: R.H. Laurie, 1839.

———. *Memoir, Descriptive and Explanatory, to Accompany the Charts of the Northern Atlantic Ocean; and comprising Instructions, General and Particular, for the Navigation of that Sea*. 10th ed. London: Printed for R.H. Laurie, 1853.

Putnam, George. *Lighthouses and Lightships of the United States*. Cambridge, MA: Riverside Press, 1917.

Reiger, George. *Wanderer on My Native Shore*. New York: Simon and Schuster, 1983.

Risk, James Russell. "Lamps, Maps, Mud-Machines, and Signal Flags: Science, Technology, and Commerce in the Early United States." Ph.D. diss, University of South Carolina, 2017.

Roales, Judith. *Delaware Lighthouses and Range Lights*. Charleston, SC: Arcadia Publishing Company, 2007.

Robinson, G.G.J., and J. Robinson. *The New Annual Register, of General Repository of History, Politics, and Literature for the Year 1785*. London, 1786.

Rose, A.W.H. *Canada in 1849: Pictures of Canadian Life; or, the Emigrant Churchman*. London: Richard Bentley, 1850.

Royle, John Forbes. *Materia Medica and Therapeutics: Including the Preparations of the Pharmacopoeias*. Philadelphia: Lea & Blanchard, 1847.

Rush, Benjamin. *Information to Europeans Who Are Disposed to Migrate to the United States*. Philadelphia: Carey, Stewart & Co., 1790.

Sanderson, Edgar. *The British Empire in the Nineteenth Century*. Vol. 1. London: Blackie & Son, Limited, 1899.

Scharf, J. Thomas. *History of Delaware*. Philadelphia: L.J. Richards & Co., 1888.

Schneider, Paul. *The Enduring Shore: A History of Cape Cod, Martha's Vineyard, and Nantucket*. New York: Henry Holt and Company, 2000.

Schomette, Donald. *Shipwrecks, Sea Raiders and Maritime Disasters Along the Delmarva Coast, 1632–2004*. Baltimore: Johns Hopkins University Press, 2007.

Schwartz, Rick. *Hurricanes and the Middle Atlantic States: A Surprising History From Jamestown to the Present*. Alexandria, VA: Blue Diamond Books, 2007.

Scott, Temple ed. *The Prose Works of Johnathan Swift, D.D.*, vol. 6, *The Drapier's Letters*. London: George Bell and Sons, 1903.

Sharp, Henry. "Artificial Beach Construction in the Vicinity of New York." *Scientific Monthly* 25, no. 1 (July 1927): 35.

Sheffield, John Lord. *Observations on the Commerce of the American States*. New York: Augustus M. Kelley, 1970.

Shepard, Birse. *Lore of the Wreckers*. Boston: Beacon Press, 1961.

Sigerson, George. *Modern Ireland: Its Vital Questions, Secret Societies and Government*. London: Longmans, Green, Reader and Dyer, 1869.

Smyth, Albert Henry. *The Writings of Benjamin Franklin*, vol. 9, *1783–1788*. New York: Macmillan Company, 1907.

Sparks, Jared. *Familiar Letters and Miscellaneous Pieces by Dr. Franklin*. Boston: Charles Bowen, 1833.

Spears, John. "Sand-Waves at Henlopen and Hatteras." *Scribner's Magazine*, July–December 1890.

Stevens, Robert White. *On the Stowage of Ships and their Cargoes*. 7th ed. New York: Longmans, Green & Co., 1894.

Stevenson, Robert Louis. *The Amateur Emigrant, From the Clyde to Sandy Hook*. New York: Charles Scribner's Sons, 1904.

Stick, David, ed. *Graveyard of the Atlantic: Shipwrecks of the North Carolina Coast*. Chapel Hill: University of North Carolina Press, 1952.

The Surf Channel. "How Heavy Are the Biggest Waves in the Ocean?" *Huffpost*, June 28, 2014. https://www.huffpost.com.

Swain, John (master shipwright). Interview with the author, August 10, 2000.

Tales of Heroism, and Register of Strange and Wonderful Adventures. London: William Mark Clark, 1847.

Tanber, George. "A Forgotten Maritime Tragedy, the Empress Sleeps in St. Lawrence." *Toledo Blade*, November 26, 2000.

Tannehill, Ivan Ray. *Hurricanes: Their Nature and History—Particularly Those of the West Indies and the Southern Coasts of the United States*. Princeton, NJ: Princeton University Press, 1943.

Thévenot, Melchisédec. *The Art of Swimming*. 3rd ed. London: John Lever, 1789.

Thomas, Ralph. *Swimming*. London: Sampson Low, Marston & Co., 1904.

Thoreau, Henry David. *Cape Cod*. New York: Thomas Y. Crowell & Co., 1908.

"Timber Bulkheads and Groins for Shore Protection at Cape Henlopen Light Station, Del." *Journal of Civil Engineering and Construction* 71 (January–June 1914): 1914.

Tone, Theobold Wolfe. *An Argument of Behalf of the Catholics of Ireland*. Reprinted by Order of the Society of United Irishmen of Belfast, 1791.

Toth, Charles. "Anglo-American Diplomacy and the British West Indies (1783–1789)." *The Americas* 32, no. 3 (1976).

Traill, Catherine Parr Strickland. *The Backwoods of Canada: Being Letters from the Wife of an Emigrant Officer*. London: Charles Knight & Co., 1846.

Trupp, Philip. *Tracking Treasure*. Washington, D.C.: Acropolis Books, 1986.

Turner, C.H.B., ed. *Some Records of Sussex County Delaware*. Philadelphia: Allen, Lane & Scott, 1909.

U.S. Army Corps of Engineers. "Indian River Inlet and Bay." July 1, 2021. https://www.nap.usace.army.mil.

U.S. Department of Agriculture, Weather Bureau. "Climatological Data: New Jersey Section." 31, no. 4 (April 1926).

U.S. Department of Commerce, National Oceanic and Atmospheric Administration. *United States Coast Pilot 3, Atlantic Coast*. 15th ed. Washington, D.C.: 1977.

U.S. Department of State. "International Convention for the Safety of Life At Sea, 1974." Opened for signature November 1, 1974. U.S. Treaties and Other International Agreements, 32 UST 197, 199 (1980).

U.S. Department of the Treasury. *Annual Report of the Light-House Board of the United States to the Secretary of the Treasury for the Fiscal Year Ending June 30, 1867*. Washington, D.C.: Government Printing Office, 1867.

———. "Letter from the Secretary of the Treasury Transmitting the Report of the General Superintendent of the Light-House Establishment, December 20, 1850." 31st Cong., 2nd Session, Ex. Doc. No. 14, 1850.

———. *Report of the Officers Constituting the Light House Board*. Washington, D.C.: A. Boyd Hamilton, 1852.

———. *Report of the Secretary of the Treasury, Communicating a Report of the Superintendent of the Survey of the Coast, Showing the Progress of the Work During the Year Ending November 1844*, December 23, 1844. 28th Congress, 2nd Session [Senate].

———. *Report of the Secretary of the Treasury on the State of the Finances, for the Year Ending June 30, 1862*. Washington, D.C.: Government Printing Office, 1863.

———. *Report of the Secretary of the Treasury on the State of the Finances for the Year 1868*. Washington, D.C.: Government Printing Office, 1868.

U.S. Life-Saving Service. *Annual Report of the Operations of the United States Life-Saving Service for the Fiscal Year Ending June 30, 1877*. Washington, D.C.: Government Printing Office, 1877.

———. *Annual Report of the Operations of the United States Life-Saving Service for the Fiscal Year Ending June 30, 1892*. Washington, D.C.: Government Printing Office, 1892.

University of Minnesota Law School, "Laws in Ireland for the Suppression of Popery Commonly Knowns as the Penal Laws." moses.law.umn.edu.

Vandeburgh, C.F. *The Mariner's Medical Guide*. London: Baldwin, Cradock and Joy, 1819.

Vanderbilt, Tom. "The Crisis in American Walking." *Slate*, April 10, 2012.

Van Doren, Carl. *Benjamin Franklin*. London: Putnam, 1939.

Webster, Noah. "Mediocrity." *An American Dictionary of the English Language*. New York: S. Converse, 1828.

Wells, Ronald. *Ulster Migration to America*. New York: Peter Lang Publishing, 1991.

Welshman, John. *Titanic: The Last Night of a Small Town*. Oxford: Oxford University Press, 2012.

Wenzel, Harry Allen. *The Ship Faithful Steward: A Story of Scots-Irish, English and Irish Migration to Pennsylvania*. Yellowtail Snapper Publishing, 2021.

Whymper, Frederick. *The Sea: Its Stirring Story of Peril, Adventure & Heroism*. London: Cassell & Company, 1883.

Wokeck, Marianne. *Trade in Strangers: The Beginnings of Mass Migration to North America*. University Park: Pennsylvania State University Press, 1999.

Wroten, William. *Assateague*. Cambridge, MD: Tidewater Publishers, 1972.

INDEX

ABOUT THE AUTHOR

Michael Timothy Dougherty served for twenty-five years in the federal government focused on law and policy. He is a former Ombudsman for Citizenship and Immigration Services and a former Assistant Secretary for Border, Immigration and Trade Policy at the U.S. Department of Homeland Security. He is a shipwreck diver. His home surf break is Indian River Inlet, Delaware.

Visit us at
www.historypress.com